CORE
SKILLS

# Test
# Preparation

**Strategies for**
- *Reading*
- *Vocabulary*
- *Math*
- *Listening*
- *Language*

Steck
Vaughn™

A Harcourt Achieve Imprint

www.Steck-Vaughn.com
1-800-531-5015

# Core Skills: Test Preparation
## Grade 1

# Contents

ISBN 0-7398-6496-3     ISBN 978-0-7398-6496-8

10 11 12 13 14 15  0982  12
4500348180

# Core Skills: Test Preparation

## Introduction

Standardized tests are becoming increasingly more important in both public and private schools, yet test anxiety causes many children to perform below their fullest potential. *Core Skills: Test Preparation* is designed to help children succeed on standardized tests. This program refreshes basic skills, familiarizes children with test formats and directions, and teaches test-taking strategies.

A large part of being well prepared for a test is knowing how to approach different types of questions and learning how to use time wisely. *Core Skills: Test Preparation* gives children the opportunity to take a test under conditions that parallel those they will face when taking standardized tests. This practice and experience will allow them to feel more confident when taking standardized tests and will enable them to demonstrate their knowledge successfully.

## Tools for Success

*Core Skills: Test Preparation* gives children valuable practice with the content areas and question formats of the major standardized tests used nationally. These include:

- CAT (California Achievement Tests)
- CTBS (Comprehensive Tests of Basic Skills)
- ITBS (Iowa Tests of Basic Skills)
- MAT (Metropolitan Achievement Tests)
- SAT (Stanford Achievement Test)

*Core Skills: Test Preparation* provides:
- Test-taking strategies
- Familiarity with test directions
- Review of skills and content
- Awareness of test formats
- Practice tests

## Organization

The book is divided into units that correspond to those found on standardized tests. These include:

- Reading Comprehension
- Reading Vocabulary and Word Study Skills
- Mathematics Problem Solving
- Listening
- Language

*Core Skills: Test Preparation* is designed to ensure success on test day by offering:

### Test-Taking Strategies
Unit 1 provides valuable test-taking strategies to help your child do his or her best on the reading portion of any standardized test.

### Targeted Reading Objectives
Unit 2 focuses on six reading objectives. Each objective contains a definition, tip, or hint to help your child master the targeted skill.

### Mathematics Problem Solving
Unit 5 offers a step-by-step approach to solving math word problems.

### Skill Lessons
The skill lessons contained in Units 3, 4, 6, 7, and 8 prepare your child by providing both content review and test-taking strategies. Each skill lesson includes:

**Directions**—clear, concise, and similar to those found on standardized tests;
A **Sample**—to familiarize children with test-taking items; and
A **Practice Section**—a set of exercises based on the lesson and modeled on the kinds of exercises found on standardized tests.

### Unit Tests
These tests cover all the skills from the lessons.

### Practice Tests
The last five units in the book, Units 9–13, are the **Practice Tests**. These tests simulate the situations that your child will encounter when taking standardized tests.

# Use

## Markers

Before beginning to work any exercises with your child, you will need to make a cardboard or paper place marker. The marker should be a rectangle that measures about 4 inches by 2 inches. The place marker will help your child keep his or her place on the page.

## Sample Questions

Each skill lesson, unit test, and practice test begins with sample questions. These questions prepare your child for the lesson or test that follows the sample. Give your child time to answer the questions, and then go over the correct answers before moving on to the lesson or test.

## Scripts

Most of the lessons, unit tests, and practice tests in this book contain scripted material that must be read aloud by an adult to the child. Adult involvement is required because many children at this age are still developing their reading skills, and scripted material prevents reading difficulties from interfering with the testing of content areas. Those sections that practice or test the child's reading ability are, of course, not scripted.

All the necessary scripts, as well as all the answers, have been collected in the section called Scripts and Answers, pages 129–172. This section has been perforated so that you can remove it easily. Your child can mark his or her answers in the book while you read from the scripted pages.

## Practice Tests

The five practice tests, pages 92–127, simulate standardized tests, providing your child with valuable practice before test day. Like standardized tests, these are timed. The following are the suggested times needed to administer each test:

| | |
|---|---|
| Reading Comprehension | 40 minutes |
| Vocabulary and Word Study Skills | 50 minutes |
| Part 1: Math Problem Solving | 40 minutes |
| Part 2: Math Procedures | 30 minutes |
| Listening | 25 minutes |
| Language | 40 minutes |

## Answer Bubbles

You may want to go over how to fill in the multiple choice bubble-in answers. Stress the importance of filling the answer bubble completely, pressing firmly, and erasing any stray marks.

## Short Answer Questions

Standardized tests also require children to answer questions using their own words. *Core Skills: Test Preparation* gives children practice answering this type of question.

## Individual Record Form

The **Individual Record Form** found on page 128 can be used to track progress through the book and to record the child's scores on the lessons, unit tests, and practice tests.

# Icons

This book contains the following icons to help you and your child:

 The **Go On** icon tells your child to continue on to the next page.

 The **Stop** icon tells your child to stop working.

 The stopwatch icon indicates the amount of time to allot for each **Practice Test**.

*Core Skills: Test Preparation* lessons and practice provide children with the tools they need to build their self-confidence. That self-confidence can translate into a positive test-taking experience and higher scores on standardized tests. With its emphasis on skills, strategies for success, and practice, *Core Skills: Test Preparation* gives children the ability to succeed on standardized tests.

Dear Parent or Educator,

Welcome to *Steck-Vaughn Core Skills: Test Preparation*. You have selected a book that will help your child develop the skills he or she needs to succeed on standardized tests.

Although testing can be a source of anxiety for children, this book will give your child the preparation and practice that he or she needs to feel better prepared and more confident when taking a standardized test. Research shows that children who are acquainted with the scoring format of standardized tests score higher on those tests. Students also score higher when they practice and understand the skills and strategies needed to take standardized tests. The subject areas and concepts presented in this book are typically found on standardized tests at this grade level.

To best help your child, please consider the following suggestions:

- Provide a quiet place to work.
- Go over the directions and the sample exercises together.
- Review the strategy tips.
- Reassure your child that the practice tests are not "real" tests.
- Encourage your child to do his or her best.
- Check the lesson when it is complete.
- Go over the answers and note improvements as well as problems.

If your child expresses anxiety about taking a test or completing these lessons, help him or her understand what causes the stress. Then, talk about ways to eliminate anxiety. Above all, enjoy this time you spend with your child: He or she will feel your support, and test scores will improve as success in test taking is experienced.

Help your child maintain a positive attitude about taking a standardized test. Let your child know that each test provides an opportunity to shine.

Sincerely,

The Educators and Staff of
Steck-Vaughn School Supply

P.S. You might want to visit our website at **www.svschoolsupply.com** for more test preparation materials as well as additional review of content areas.

# Standardized Test Content Areas

## Reading Skills

Recognizing and identifying words that tell about pictures

Identifying compound words

Identifying sounds in word endings, recognizing suffixes

Identifying contractions

Recognizing and matching consonant sounds, consonant blends, consonant digraphs, short and long vowel sounds, vowel diphthongs, vowel digraphs, and r-controlled vowels

Recognizing rhyming sounds

Using pictures to solve riddles

Relating pictures to words and sentences

Identifying the main idea

Recalling specific details

Making inferences

Drawing conclusions

Extending meaning

Understanding actions, reasons, and sequence

Understanding cause and effect

Predicting outcomes

Using definitional phrases to determine word meanings

Relating pictures to stories

Identifying sequence

## Language Skills

Listening to remember stated details, sequences, and directions

Drawing conclusions

Making inferences

Matching pictures that rhyme with words to complete poems

Distinguishing between reality and fantasy

Determining the purpose for writing

Determining appropriate topic and topic relevance

Organizing information and ideas

Alphabetizing words

Using the parts of a book to locate information

Determining correct sentence order

Identifying extraneous information in paragraphs

Identifying correctly applied grammar

Identifying correct capitalization and punctuation

Identifying correctly and effectively written sentences

Identifying misspelled words in sentences

Recognizing the misspellings of sight words

## Mathematics Skills

Understanding numeration and number systems

Identifying ordinal position

Comparing and ordering numbers

Understanding expanded notation and place value

Finding place value

Identifying the identity element for addition

Identifying the inverse operation

Identifying fractional parts of a whole

Counting

Reading and interpreting pictographs, tables, and tally charts

Determining simple probability

Identifying geometric shapes and patterns

Understanding basic properties of plane, congruent, and symmetrical figures

Identifying components of geometric figures

Using standard and nonstandard units to estimate and to measure

Identifying appropriate measurement units

Telling time to the nearest half-hour

Reading a calendar to locate information

Counting and trading coins and determining their value

Identifying number sentences that represent pictures

Identifying arithmetic operations

Using non-routine strategies to solve problems

Applying addition and subtraction to word problems

Adding and subtracting whole numbers

# Reading: Test-Taking Strategies

These steps will help you do your best on reading tests. They will help you find out what you need to know to answer the questions.

## STRATEGY 1
### The CHECK AND SEE Strategy

These steps can be used when a question asks for a fact from the story. The answer to the question is in the story. It is not hidden. Some of the same words may be in the story and in the question.

**Check and See** will help you answer questions that ask you to *remember* things.

---

**This is the Check and See Strategy**

1. READ: **Read** the question.

2. FIND: **Find** the words you need in the story.

3. CHOOSE: **Choose** which strategy to use.
   **Check and See:** Put a **check** next to the sentence where you can **see** the words you need to answer the question.

4. ANSWER: Pick the best **answer**.

---

▶GO ON▶

## STRATEGY 2
### The PUZZLE PIECE Strategy
These steps can be used when a question asks you what something means. Sometimes there does not seem to be an answer. It is not found in the story.

**Puzzle Piece** helps you put facts together. This is like putting a puzzle together. Puzzles are made up of many pieces. You cannot look at one piece and know what the picture is. Only when you put the pieces together can you see the whole picture.

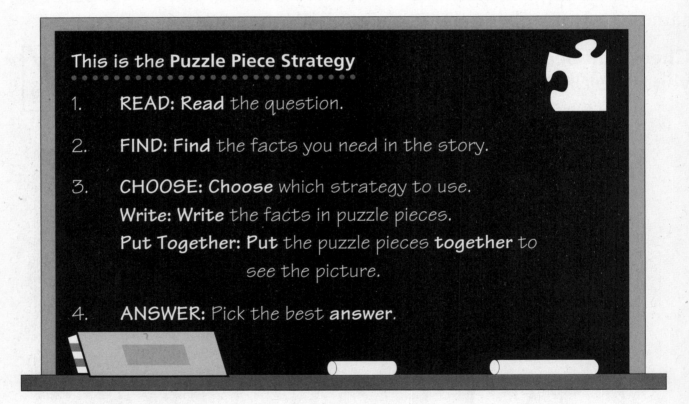

**This is the Puzzle Piece Strategy**

1.    READ: **Read** the question.

2.    FIND: **Find** the facts you need in the story.

3.    CHOOSE: **Choose** which strategy to use.
      Write: **Write** the facts in puzzle pieces.
      Put Together: **Put** the puzzle pieces **together** to see the picture.

4.    ANSWER: Pick the best **answer**.

▶GO ON

# STRATEGY 3
## The WHAT LIGHTS UP Strategy

These are other steps you can use when an answer is not in the story. You need to add your own ideas to the story.

**What Lights Up** can help you see if something is real, useful, or a fact. It can show you what would happen if the story had a different ending.

You can use the **What Lights Up** Strategy to answer the hardest type of question. This is when you are asked to read and think of your own ideas.

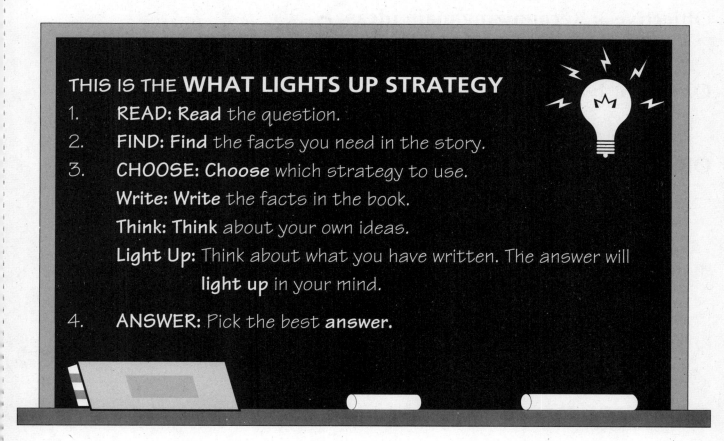

THIS IS THE **WHAT LIGHTS UP STRATEGY**

1.    READ: **Read** the question.
2.    FIND: **Find** the facts you need in the story.
3.    CHOOSE: **Choose** which strategy to use.

   **Write: Write** the facts in the book.

   **Think: Think** about your own ideas.

   **Light Up:** Think about what you have written. The answer will **light up** in your mind.

4.    ANSWER: Pick the best **answer.**

# Reading Comprehension

## Specific Objectives

**Objective 1: Determining word meanings**
*Context clues*

**Objective 2: Identifying supporting ideas**
*Recalling facts and details and sequential order*

**Objective 3: Recognizing main ideas**
*Stated main ideas*

**Objective 4: Perceiving relationships and recognizing outcomes**
*Cause-and-effect and making predictions*

**Objective 5: Making inferences and generalizations**
*Inferring information and drawing conclusions*

GO ON

# Specific Objectives

## Objective 1: Determining Word Meanings

**Sometimes you can find out the meaning of a new word by using the words around it as clues.**

The new shoes did not fit. They were the <u>wrong</u> size.

1 **In this paragraph, the word <u>wrong</u> means —**

   ○ too big.

   ◉ not right.

   ○ the same.

*Hint: You get a clue about the word <u>wrong</u> by reading the words "did not fit."*

David won <u>first</u> prize in the spelling bee. He spelled every word right.

2 **In this paragraph, the word <u>first</u> means —**

   ◉ the best.

   ○ in front.

   ○ before.

*Hint: You get a clue about the word <u>first</u> by reading the next sentence.*

▶GO ON

Sula cannot find her brother. She peeked into his room to see if he was there.

The teacher wanted her book back. She asked if I had finished reading it yet.

**3** **In this paragraph, the word peeked means —**

   ○ called.

   ◉ looked.

   ○ walked.

*Hint: You get a clue about the word peeked by reading the whole sentence.*

**4** **In this paragraph, the word finished means —**

   ○ still.

   ○ liked.

   ◉ done.

*Hint: You get a clue about the word finished by the word "yet" and by reading both sentences.*

GO ON

The school bus came to a <u>stop</u>. There was a red light.

**5** In this paragraph, the word <u>stop</u> means —

○ get on.

○ get off.

◉ wait.

*Hint: You get a clue about the word <u>stop</u> by looking at the next sentence.*

Ming turned the wheel. We watched it <u>spin</u>.

**6** In this paragraph, the word <u>spin</u> means —

◉ go around.

○ roll away.

○ go for a ride.

*Hint: You get a clue about the word <u>spin</u> by reading the first sentence.*

GO ON

The teacher did not want us to run. She told us to walk <u>slowly</u>.

**7** **In this paragraph, the word <u>slowly</u> means —**

○ at once.

◉ not fast.

○ not slow.

*Hint: You get a clue about what <u>slowly</u> means by reading the first sentence.*

Marta's job was to <u>greet</u> people. She stood at the door as they came into the room. She was smiling.

**8** **In this paragraph, the word <u>greet</u> means —**

◉ to say hello.

○ to say good-bye.

○ to check.

*Hint: You get a clue about what <u>greet</u> means by reading the last two sentences.*

STOP

# Objective 2: Identifying Supporting Ideas

**Facts and ideas are important. By finding them, you will know what the story is about.**

Tina and her family went to the beach last summer. One day, they went to see a lighthouse.

Mr. Beal, the man who worked at the lighthouse, told Tina all about it. The lighthouse is 90 years old. It is all white and it is 120 feet tall. It has a strong light. Sailors can see the light as far as 24 miles out at sea.

**1  Tina and her family went to —**

○ the city.

○ the beach.

○ the country.

*Hint: Look at the first sentence.*

**2  Who is Mr. Beal?**

○ a sailor

○ Tina's father

○ the man who works at the lighthouse

*Hint: Read the second paragraph.*

**3  How tall is the lighthouse?**

○ 90 feet

○ 120 feet

○ 24 feet

*Hint: Look for the sentence that talks about how tall the lighthouse is.*

GO ON

Have you ever looked closely at the top of a tree stump? You might see many rings. The rings are often narrow near the center of the tree and wider near the outside.

Each ring stands for a year of growth. As a tree grows, more and more rings are added. After the tree has been cut down, you can see the rings on the stump. The number of rings tells the tree's age. The more rings you count, the older the tree is.

**4** **What part of the tree should you look at to find its age?**

○ the branches

○ the stump

○ the bark

*Hint: Read the first paragraph.*

**5** **The tree's rings are all**

○ the same size.

○ narrow.

○ different sizes.

*Hint: Look at the third sentence.*

**6** **What can you say about a tree with many rings?**

○ It is old.

○ It is young.

○ It is tall.

*Hint: Look at the last sentence.*

▶GO ON

# Objective 2: Identifying Supporting Ideas

**It is helpful to put events in the order they happened. This may help you to understand a passage.**

"What's the matter, Lucy?" asked her teacher.

"I lost my new gloves. I looked everywhere, but I can't find them."

When it was time to go home, Lucy put on her coat. She put her hands in her pockets. Then she started to smile. There in her pockets were her gloves, just where she had left them.

**1 Which of these happened first in the story?**

- ○ Lucy found her gloves.
- ◉ Lucy lost her gloves.
- ○ Lucy looked for her gloves.

*Hint: Look at the beginning of the story.*

**2 When did Lucy put on her coat?**

- ◉ when it was time to go home
- ○ when Lucy lost her gloves
- ○ when Lucy looked for her gloves

*Hint: Look at the last paragraph.*

**3 Which of these happened last in the story?**

- ◉ Lucy put her hands in her pockets.
- ○ Lucy told the teacher she couldn't find her gloves.
- ○ Lucy found her gloves.

*Hint: Look at the last paragraph.*

▶ GO ON

Yuko and Rosa were playing outside. They saw a dog across the street. Just then Mr. Jackson came outside.

"Look at that poor little dog, Mr. Jackson. He looks hungry. What can we do to help him?" asked Yuko.

"I'll get him some food," said Mr. Jackson. He went inside and came back out with some food for the dog.

4 **Which of these happened first in the story?**

○ Mr. Jackson gave the dog some food.

◉ Yuko and Rosa were playing outside.

○ The girls saw a dog.

*Hint: Look at the beginning of the story.*

5 **When did Mr. Jackson get the dog some food?**

○ when he saw the girls playing outside

○ when his sister asked him to

◉ when the girls asked him for help

*Hint: Look at the second paragraph.*

6 **Which of these happened last in the story?**

○ The dog was given food.

○ Yuko and Rosa saw a dog.

◉ Mr. Jackson came outside.

*Hint: Look at the end of the story.*

STOP

# Objective 3: Recognizing Main Ideas

**The main idea is the meaning of the story. Many times it is stated in the story.**

Did you know that some birds could talk? Some parrots can talk. They say what they hear. Sometimes, they say things at the wrong time.

I have a parrot. It was a birthday present. My parrot says many things. One day, my mother was telling me to pick up my toys. The parrot said, "Be quiet!" Mom gave me a funny look. She told me to clean my room. "Be quiet!" said the parrot.

Mom got so angry that she told me to stay in my room for the rest of the day.

**1** **What is the main idea of this story?**

○ Parrots make great gifts.

○ It is important to keep your room clean.

◉ Parrots can say things at the wrong time.

*Hint: Think about the whole story. Look at the first paragraph.*

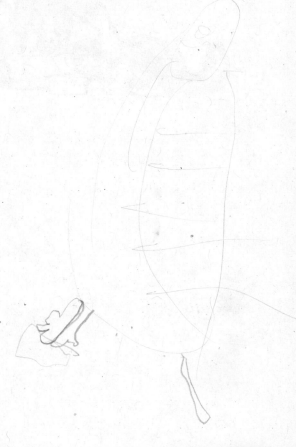

▶ GO ON ▶

Ricka says she wants to be an animal doctor. She loves all kinds of animals. She has three pets. She has two dogs and one cat.

Ricka takes care of all her pets. She makes sure that they eat well. She sees that they get plenty of rest and play. She brushes their fur. She does everything the animal doctor tells her to do.

I think that Ricka will be a good animal doctor one day.

**2  What is the main idea of this story?**

○  Ricka takes care of her three pets.

◉  Ricka wants to be an animal doctor.

○  Ricka listens to the animal doctor.

*Hint: What does the whole story talk about?*

Ricka and her pets

STOP

16

# Objective 4: Perceiving Relationships and Recognizing Outcomes

**Knowing what happened (effect) and what made it happen (cause) helps you to understand what you read.**

After Kenji was born, Grandma came to visit from Japan. She met my new brother, Kenji, for the first time. I think she likes him better than she likes me.

Everyone in my family likes Kenji because he is so cute. They talk about him all day. I like him, too, but I want my family to like me again. I came first. I am five years old. I have a lot to talk about. Kenji cannot talk. He just sleeps all day.

**1  Why did Grandma come to visit?**

○   She wanted to move from Japan.

◉   She wanted to see the new baby.

○   She wanted to take a trip.

*Hint: What happened that made Grandma come to visit?*

**2  Why does everyone like Kenji?**

◉   He's a cute little baby.

○   He is the first child.

○   He sleeps a lot.

*Hint: What is it about Kenji that everyone likes?*

GO ON

Julia could not run very fast. She could not run as fast as the others. She wanted to do better. Every day she tried running faster and faster. Soon she was able to run so fast that she won a race. She was very happy.

**3  Why does Julia run every day?**

○  She is happy.

○  She likes to run.

◉  She wants to run faster.

*Hint: What makes Julia run every day?*

**4  Why is Julia happy?**

◉  She won a race.

○  It is her birthday.

○  She cannot run as fast as the others.

*Hint: What made Julia happy at the end of the story?*

▶GO ON

# Objective 4: Perceiving Relationships and Recognizing Outcomes

**Sometimes you can tell what might happen next. You must think about what would make sense if the story were to go on.**

Tricia cannot decide how to spend her money. She got ten dollars for her birthday. She has had the money a month. She has not spent it yet. There are many things she wants to buy.

She wants to buy a book. She likes books with many pretty pictures. She likes books about animals.

She wants to buy a puzzle, too. She likes the ones with many pieces. She spreads the pieces all over the floor. It takes a long time to finish it.

**1 What will happen next?**
- ○ Tricia will buy some stuffed animals.
- ○ Tricia will ask for some more money.
- ◉ Tricia will buy a book or a puzzle.

*Hint: Think about what Tricia wants to buy with her money.*

GO ON

Mia's aunt likes to collect things. She collects tiny glass animals. She has two dogs and three cats all made of glass. She has them on a shelf above her table. They are pretty to look at.

Mia's aunt also collects dolls. She has many dolls. Some of them wear fancy costumes. They come from many different countries.

Mia's aunt is coming to visit next week. Mia would like to buy her something.

**2 What will Mia do tomorrow?**

○ visit her aunt

◉ go shopping for a gift

○ stay home from school

*Hint: Read the last paragraph.*

STOP

# Objective 5: Making Inferences and Generalizations

**What a character says and thinks tells you what that person feels.**

Patrick thinks his cat should have a collar. His cat likes to go outside. Sometimes the cat is gone for a long time. What if the cat cannot find his way home? Patrick decides to buy his cat a collar. Patrick's name and phone number will be on the collar. The cat's name will be on the collar, too.

**1 Why does Patrick want his cat to have a new collar?**

○ The cat will be happier with one.

◉ He is afraid his cat will get lost.

○ The collar he has now is very old.

*Hint: Why is Patrick worried?*

▶ GO ON

Maine is a great place to visit. You can go swimming in the ocean. There are sandy beaches. There are many mountains too. You can go walking in the woods. You can climb up the mountains. When you get to the top you can see things far away. There are many fun things to do in Maine.

**2 What do you know about the boy telling this story?**

○ He likes to play baseball.

○ He is a good swimmer.

○ He likes to go to Maine.

*Hint: Read the whole story. Look at the first and last sentences.*

STOP

## Solving Riddles

**Sample A**

I cannot fly.
I can sing.

○   ○   ○

**1**

I can be seen in the sky.
I can be seen at night.

○   ○   ○

**2**

I live in the ocean.
I have sharp teeth.

  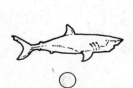  

○   ○   ○

**3**

It has wheels.
It is a toy.

○   ○   ○

**4**

It floats in the water.
You sit in it.

○   ○   ○

**5**

It gives light.
It is hot.

○   ○   ○

# Completing Sentences

## Sample

**A** **Sheila found some**

    trees      bees      grass

    ○       ●       ○

**B** **She is**

    walking   dancing   running

    ○       ○       ○

**4** **Julio is making**

    salad     soup   pancakes

    ○       ●       ○

**5** **He is wearing a cook's**

    hat      sign     coat

    ○       ○       ○

**STOP**

**1** **Cara is sitting on her mother's**

    lap      bed     chair

    ○       ○       ○

**2** **Her mother is reading her a**

    letter  newspaper  book

    ○       ○       ○

**3** **Soon Cara will**

    wake up   play    sleep

    ○       ○       ○

**6** **Andy could not find his**

    shoe   brother   pet

    ○       ○       ●

**7** **Andy looked under his**

    bed     desk   pillow

    ○       ○       ○

**8** **There he found his**

    rabbit   turtle   duck

    ○       ●       ○

**STOP**

## Sample A
## Our Toy Boats

We each have a toy boat. Marta has a red boat. Ben's boat is blue. My boat is yellow.

**What color is Ben's boat?**

○ red

○ blue

○ yellow

**STOP**

---

## Manny Helps Out

Manny likes to help his family. He is only four years old. He thinks he can do things his big brother can do. He wants to help his dad. His dad is painting the house. His dad gives Manny paint and a brush.

Manny gets paint all over his clothes. Dad says, "You will do better when you are five." Manny says, "I don't want to paint anymore. I want to have some fun." Dad laughs.

**1 Manny's brother is**

○ older than Manny.

○ younger than Manny.

○ the same age as Manny.

**2 Why does Manny want to paint the house?**

○ He is a good painter.

○ He wants to help his dad.

○ He does not like the color of the house.

**3 What happens to Manny's clothes?**

○ He tears them.

○ He washes them.

○ He gets paint on them.

**4 What might happen next in the story?**

○ Manny will paint more.

○ Manny will go out to play.

○ Manny will wash all of his clothes.

**GO ON**

## Playing with Blocks

Bess has a set of blocks. Her blocks are red, blue, and green. She builds many things with her blocks. One day she built a blue block house. Another day she built a car of red blocks. Sometimes her block buildings fall down. Then she feels sad. She has to start building all over again.

**5** **You can tell that Bess likes to**
- ○ color things.
- ○ build things.
- ○ knock things down.

**6** **What did Bess build with red blocks?**

_____

_ _ _ _ _ _ _ _ _ _ _ _ _ _ _ _ _ _ _

_____

**7** **How does Bess feel when the blocks fall?**
- ○ unhappy
- ○ angry
- ○ afraid

**8** **This story tells how Bess**
- ○ draws pictures.
- ○ sings songs.
- ○ plays with blocks.

GO ON

# Lila's Party

Lila wanted to have a party for the end of school. Her dad helped her write notes to her friends.

Please come to an End of the Year Party Saturday, June 10, from 2:00 to 4:00 P.M. at City Park. First we will swim, then we will eat pizza. If you can come, please call Lila at 555-5565. Hope to see you at the park!

**9 Why is Lila having a party?**
- ○ It is her birthday.
- ○ It is the end of school.
- ○ It is the Fourth of July.

**10 What will Lila and her friends eat at the party?**

_____

\- - - - - - - - - - - - - - - - -

_____

**11 What should Lila's friends bring to the party?**
- ○ a swimsuit
- ○ books
- ○ a birthday present

**12 What should her friends do if they can come?**
- ○ write a note to Lila
- ○ call Lila
- ○ call their teacher

▶ GO ON

# Peppy

We have a new dog at our house. His name is Peppy. He is two years old. My sister and I like to play with Peppy. We throw a ball, and he brings it back. We take him for walks on our street. Peppy barks when he is hungry. I put food in his bowl. My sister gives him cool water. We take good care of Peppy.

**13  How old is Peppy?**

_____

_____

_____

**14  You can tell that the children**
- ○  are unhappy with Peppy.
- ○  love Peppy.
- ○  are afraid of Peppy.

**15  When does Peppy bark?**
- ○  when he wants food
- ○  when he goes for a walk
- ○  when he is tired

**16  This story tells about**
- ○  two children and their new pet.
- ○  a man and his cat.
- ○  how to find a dog.

STOP

**Sample A**

I can bark.
I cannot run.

○      ○      ○

**STOP**

**1** I can smile.
I cannot walk.

○      ○      ○

**2** It can fly.
It takes people places.

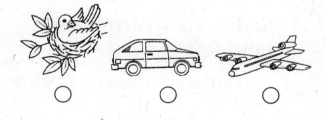

○      ○      ○

**3** I can play games.
I wear clothes.

○      ○      ○

**4** It is green.
It is an animal.

○      ○      ○

**5** It is silver.
You can eat with it.

○      ○      ○

**6** It is hot.
You plug it in.

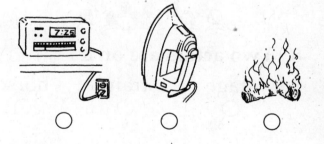

○      ○      ○

**7** It is clothing.
It is worn on the feet.

○      ○      ○

**STOP**

**Sample**

**B  Ming and Elly are on the**

    beach      floor      table
     ○         ○        ○

**C  They are**

    walking   sleeping   playing
     ○        ○       ○

**STOP**

**8  Two actors are on a**

    stage     train     horse
    ○       ○      ○

**9  The people watching will**

    sing     talk     clap
    ○      ○     ○

**10  They will leave when the play is**

    over   beginning  written
    ○      ○     ○

**11  Ted and Luis are putting up a**

    table   house   tent
    ○     ○     ○

**12  Soon they will be**

    finished  arriving  rested
    ○     ○     ○

**13  Sadako is wearing her mother's**

    coat   dress  gloves
    ○     ○     ○

**14  She is having a lot of**

    trouble  visitors  fun
    ○     ○     ○

**15  Sadako is**

    talking  crying  smiling
    ○     ○     ○

**STOP**

## Sample D
## Baseball Game

Marc throws the ball. Sue Lin hits the ball. Juan chases the ball.

**Who hits the ball?**

○ Marc

○ Sue Lin

○ Juan

## Rita's Find

One day Rita found a baby bird in the yard. There was no nest nearby. There was no mother bird.

Rita picked up the tiny bird. She kept it for three weeks. The bird grew strong.

Rita took the bird outside. It flew to a nearby tree. It began to sing. Rita knew that her bird would be fine.

**16  Where did Rita find the bird?**

_____

- - - - - - - - - - - - - - - -

_____

**17  Why did Rita take care of the bird?**

○ Its mother was gone.

○ She liked to sing.

○ Rita's teacher told her to keep it.

**18  Why did the bird fly to a nearby tree?**

○ It wanted to hide.

○ It saw its mother.

○ It was ready to take care of itself.

**19  You can tell that Rita is**

○ kind.

○ silly.

○ unhappy.

GO ON

# Elephants

Have you ever seen an elephant? The elephant has a very long nose. It is called a trunk. The elephant's trunk weighs about 300 pounds. Elephants can use their trunks to smell. Elephants use their trunks to hold things, too. They can hold up to 600 pounds. Elephants also use their trunks to reach food. Their trunks help them grab leaves high up in trees. They pull grasses from the ground. Elephants use their trunks in many ways.

**20  What is an elephant's nose called?**

- ○ a beak
- ○ a bill
- ○ a trunk

**21  How many pounds can elephants hold with their trunks?**

_____

- - - - - - - - - - - - - - - - - - - - -

_____

**22  This story tells some ways that elephants**

- ○ take baths.
- ○ use their trunks.
- ○ take care of their babies.

**23  For an elephant, the trunk is very**

- ○ important.
- ○ dusty.
- ○ light.

GO ON

## The Springtown Puppets

Sophie and Max wanted to put on a puppet show. They practiced their show and found a place to have it. The next morning they put up signs at the community center and at the park.

> Puppet show today!
> Come to Springtown
> Community Center.
> Show time at 3:30 P.M.
> No charge to watch the show.

**24** **Where will the puppet show be held?**

- ○ Springtown Community Center
- ○ the park
- ○ Sophie's house

**25** **What time does the puppet show begin?**

_____

- - - - - - - - - - - - - - - -

_____

**26** **How much does it cost to go to the puppet show?**

- ○ It costs 50¢.
- ○ It costs 75¢.
- ● It is free.

GO ON

## The Old Man's New Friend

Long ago there was an old man. He lived by himself in a little house in the forest. Sometimes he was afraid to be alone. One day he found a unicorn at his door. The unicorn had a hurt leg. The man felt sorry for the animal. So he led the unicorn inside and took care of its leg. Then he gave the unicorn some warm milk. The unicorn thanked the man. It said, "I will stay and keep you safe." The man was never afraid again.

**27** **The man lived in**
- ○ a city.
- ○ a cave.
- ◉ a forest.

**28** **How did the man help the unicorn?**
- ○ He took it to the doctor.
- ◉ He fixed its leg and fed it.
- ○ He washed and brushed it.

**29** **Why was the man never afraid again?**
- ◉ The unicorn stayed with the man.
- ○ The man moved away.
- ○ The man talked to animals.

**30** **You can tell that the unicorn was**
- ◉ thankful.
- ○ funny.
- ○ afraid.

STOP

# Vocabulary and Word Study Skills

## Matching Words to Pictures

**Sample**

**A**  duck ○    dog ◉    doll ○

**B**  stairs ○    large ○    ladder ◉

🛑 STOP

**1**  boy ◉    bread ○    lady ○

**2**  shopping ◉    walking ○    jumping ○

**3**  friends ○    foods ◉    toys ○

**4**  child ◉    man ○    pony ○

**5**  throw ○    borrow ○    bounce ◉

**6**  rope ○    block ○    ball ◉

**7**  water ○    chop ○    plant ◉

**8**  treasure ○    tree ◉    vegetables ○

**9**  shovel ○    hammer ○    nail ○

**10**  hiding ○    left ○    rake ◉

**11**  leaves ◉    back ○    holding ○

**12**  loaves ○    helping ◉    red ○

**13**  gate ○    door ◉    fence ○

**14**  stamps ○    trees ○    steps ◉

**15**  leave ◉    learn ○    over ○

🛑 STOP

# Recognizing Compound Words

## Sample A
- ● sometimes
- ○ counting
- ○ hammer

🛑 STOP

## 1
- ● peanut
- ○ pepper
- ○ powder

Peanut.

## 2
- ○ fishing
- ● tugboat
- ○ window

## 3
- ● football
- ○ looked
- ○ backing

## 4
- ○ pitcher
- ● sundown
- ○ happy

## 5
- ○ teacher
- ● outside
- ○ weather

## 6
- ○ memory
- ● airplane
- ○ answer

## 7
- ○ fellow
- ○ missing
- ● daylight

🛑 STOP

# Choosing Correct Words

**Sample A**

- ● rained
- ○ raining
- ○ rains

🛑

**1**

- ● sang
- ○ singing
- ○ sings

**2**

- ○ reads
- ● reading
- ○ read

**3**

- ○ branch
- ○ branching
- ○ branches

**4**

- ○ sleep
- ● sleepy
- ○ sleeping

**5**

- ● bakes
- ○ baking
- ○ baked

**6**

- ○ dances
- ○ dancing
- ● dance

**7**

- ○ high
- ● higher
- ○ highest

**8**

- ○ flash
- ○ flashed
- ○ flashing

**9**

- ○ lowest
- ○ low
- ○ lower

🛑

# Recognizing Contractions

**Sample A**

- ⊙ I'd
- ○ I've
- ○ I'm

🛑STOP

**1**

- ○ we'll
- ○ we've
- ○ we're

**2**

- ○ she'd
- ○ she'll
- ○ she's

**3**

- ○ who's
- ○ who'll
- ○ who'd

**4**

- ○ we're
- ○ we'll
- ○ we'd ✓

**5**

- ○ haven't
- ○ hadn't
- ○ hasn't ✓

**6**

- ○ weren't
- ○ won't
- ○ wasn't

**7**

- ○ you'll
- ○ you'd ✓
- ○ you've

🛑STOP

# Matching Word Sounds

**Sample A**

**fi<u>sh</u>**

| pond | dish | dinner |
|:---:|:---:|:---:|
| ○ | ○ | ○ |

**STOP**

**1  l<u>i</u>ft**

| kind | pin | light |
|:---:|:---:|:---:|
| ○ | ○ | ○ |

**2  hi<u>d</u>**

| lip | ring | mad |
|:---:|:---:|:---:|
| ○ | ○ | ○ |

**3  <u>c</u>at**

| cent | kitten | hat |
|:---:|:---:|:---:|
| ○ | ○ | ○ |

**4  pa<u>th</u>**

| third | where | chair |
|:---:|:---:|:---:|
| ○ | ○ | ○ |

**5  <u>t</u>en**

| laps | deep | today |
|:---:|:---:|:---:|
| ○ | ○ | ○ |

**6  l<u>i</u>ght**

| bite | wish | list |
|:---:|:---:|:---:|
| ○ | ○ | ○ |

**7  <u>ch</u>ase**

| watch | farm | hold |
|:---:|:---:|:---:|
| ○ | ○ | ○ |

**8  tr<u>ai</u>n**

| plane | track | fine |
|:---:|:---:|:---:|
| ○ | ○ | ○ |

**9  f<u>a</u>ce**

| state | part | straw |
|:---:|:---:|:---:|
| ○ | ○ | ○ |

**STOP**

# Recognizing Consonant Sounds

**Sample A**

○    ○    ○

**STOP**

**Sample B**

choice    witch    pitcher
○          ○        ○

**STOP**

**1**

○    ○    ○

**2**

○    ○    ○

**3**

what    hatch    trip
○       ○        ○

**4**

this    time    tank
○       ○       ○

**5**

○    ○    ○

**6**

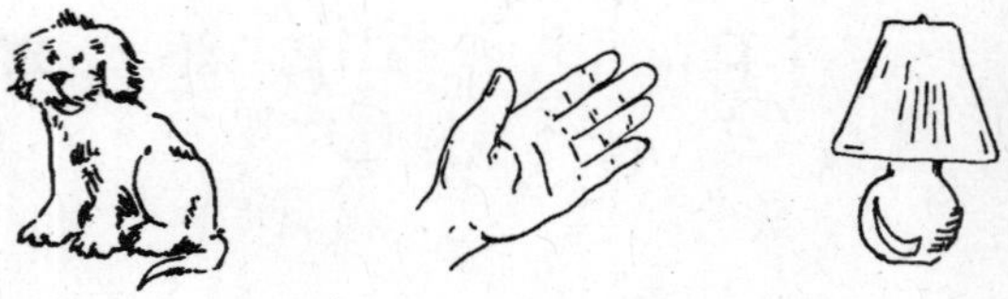

○    ○    ○

**7**

silly    missing    class
○        ○          ○

**8**

leave    jelly    nibble
○        ○        ○

**STOP**

# Identifying Rhyming Sounds

**Sample A**

○ ○ ○

**STOP**

**1**

○ ○ ○

**2**

○ ○ ○

**3**

soup     chop     flop

○ ○ ○

**4**

chase     race     days

○ ○ ○

**5**

○ ○ ○

**6**

○ ○ ○

**7**

hand     lamb     bank

○ ○ ○

**8**

should     show     shout

○ ○ ○

**9**

camp     lamb     land

○ ○ ○

**STOP**

41

# Using Endings to Build New Words

**Sample A**

fail

| ous | ness | ing |
|---|---|---|
| ○ | ○ | ◉ |

STOP

**1 cheer**

| ful | ly | est |
|---|---|---|
| ◉ | ○ | ○ |

**2 perfect**

| some | like | ly |
|---|---|---|
| ○ | ○ | ◉ |

**3 smooth**

| er | ous | hood |
|---|---|---|
| ◉ | ○ | ○ |

**4 sad**

| ness | ing | ed |
|---|---|---|
| ◉ | ○ | ○ |

**5 final**

| ing | ful | ly |
|---|---|---|
| ○ | ○ | ◉ |

**6 perform**

| some | er | like |
|---|---|---|
| ○ | ◉ | ○ |

**7 enjoy**

| able | less | ful |
|---|---|---|
| ◉ | ○ | ○ |

**8 great**

| ness | ish | less |
|---|---|---|
| ◉ | ○ | ○ |

**9 fool**

| ly | ish | ness |
|---|---|---|
| ○ | ◉ | ○ |

**10 joy**

| ing | ness | ful |
|---|---|---|
| ○ | ○ | ◉ |

STOP

**Sample**

| | | | | | 7 | rainbow ○ | sun ○ | rain ● |
|---|---|---|---|---|---|---|---|---|

**A** doctor ○   dragon ●   horse ○

**B** fire ○   water ○   smoke ●

**C** costume ●   crowd ○   coat ○

**STOP**

7  rainbow ○   sun ○   rain ●

8  clouds ●   clowns ○   stars ○

9  bright ○   storm ●   store ○

**1** pull ●   too ○   put ○

**2** worm ○   wagon ●   bike ○

**3** party ○   old ○   puppy ●

**10** leaf ○   lady ●   pet ○

**11** barn ○   belt ○   bowl ●

**12** shake ○   stir ●   wash ○

**4** dry ○   wash ●   break ○

**5** ice ○   soap ●   soup ○

**6** dishes ●   clothes ○   floor ○

**13** evening ○   picnic ●   frame ○

**14** eating ●   picture ○   baking ○

**15** nickel ○   friends ●   fresh ○

**STOP**

## Sample D

- ○ fiddle
- ○ rather
- ◉ bedroom

STOP

**16**

- ◉ teacup
- ○ picked
- ○ ringing

**17**

- ○ sadly
- ○ kicking
- ◉ raincoat

**18**

- ◉ anyone
- ○ yellow
- ○ painter

**19**

- ○ mopping
- ◉ seashell
- ○ table

STOP

## Sample E

- ◉ coldest
- ○ colder
- ○ cold

STOP

**20**

- ◉ clearly
- ○ clear
- ○ clearest

**21**

- ○ care
- ○ careless
- ◉ careful

**22**

- ◉ quickly
- ○ quicker
- ○ quick

**23**

- ○ friend
- ◉ friendly
- ○ friends

STOP

## Sample F
- ○ hadn't
- ● haven't
- ○ hasn't

🛑 STOP

**24**
- ● isn't
- ○ wasn't
- ○ aren't

**25**
- ● that's
- ○ what's
- ○ where's

**26**
- ○ he's
- ○ he'll
- ● he'd

**27**
- ○ they've
- ○ they'd
- ● they're

🛑 STOP

## Sample G
**broom**

| brand | black | best |
|-------|-------|------|
| ● | ○ | ○ |

🛑 STOP

**28 good**

| food | book | coat |
|------|------|------|
| ● | ○ | ○ |

**29 shower**

| cool | rope | loud |
|------|------|------|
| ○ | ○ | ● |

**30 tear**

| every | brother | wear |
|-------|---------|------|
| ○ | ○ | ● |

**31 cream**

| never | beg | week |
|-------|-----|------|
| ○ | ○ | ● |

🛑 STOP

## Sample H

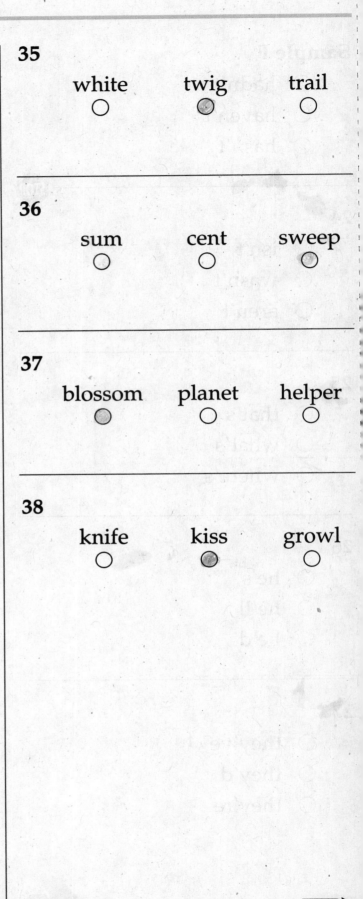

**STOP**

**32**

**33**

**34**

float    roar    front
○        ○       ●

**35**

white    twig    trail
○        ●       ○

**36**

sum      cent    sweep
○        ○       ●

**37**

blossom  planet  helper
●        ○       ○

**38**

knife    kiss    growl
○        ●       ○

▶ **GO ON**

**39**

     2    

◉     ○     ○

**40**

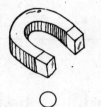          7

○     ○     ○

**41**

○     ○     ○

**42**

chief     found     reach
○     ○     ○

**43**

bird     dance     fold
○     ○     ○

**44**

gentle     wagon     cracker
○     ○     ○

**45**

sadden     listen     mailed
○     ○     ○

**46**

lesson     noisy     finish
○     ○     ○

🛑 STOP

47

## Sample I

○       ○       ○

🛑 **STOP**

**47**

○       ○       ○

**48**

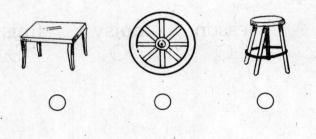

○       ○       ○

**49**

near     clear     bear
○       ○       ○

**50**

face     ways     case
○       ○       ○

**51**

good     flood     food
○       ○       ○

**52**

bead     plead     head
○       ○       ○

**53**

shoe     snow     slow
○       ○       ○

**54**

drown     damp     clam
○       ○       ○

🛑 **STOP**

**Sample J**

**fear**

   ly        less        ness
   ○         ○         ○

**STOP**

---

**55  hope**

   ful        ed        ly
   ○         ○         ○

---

**56  dark**

   ed        er        ing
   ○         ○         ○

---

**57  follow**

   ly        ous        ing
   ○         ○         ○

**58  scold**

   ity        est        ing
   ○         ○         ○

---

**59  rough**

   ter        est        ful
   ○         ○         ○

---

**60  laugh**

   ed        ly        est
   ○         ○         ○

---

**61  sing**

   ed        est        er
   ○         ○         ○

**STOP**

# Math: Problem-Solving Strategies

## Overview
## The Problem-Solving Plan

*Here are the steps to do problems:*

**STEP 1:** **WHAT IS THE QUESTION?**
Read the problem. Can you see what you must find?
What is being asked?

**STEP 2:** **FIND THE FACTS**
Find the facts:
**A.** IMPORTANT FACTS . . . You need these to do the problem.
**B.** FACTS YOU DON'T NEED . . . Some facts are not needed to do the problem.
**C.** MORE FACTS NEEDED . . . Do you need more facts to do the problem?

**STEP 3:** **GET A PLAN**
Choose a way to do the problem.

**STEP 4:** **DO THE PROBLEM**
Use your plan to do the problem.

**STEP 5:** **DOES YOUR ANSWER MAKE SENSE?**
Read the problem again.
Does your answer make sense?

▶ GO ON

## PROBLEM/QUESTION:

Tania wants to buy a new fish tank. The one in the store can hold up to 15 fish. She has 6 goldfish and 5 guppies. Will this tank be large enough for all her fish?

**STEP 1:  WHAT IS THE QUESTION?**

**STEP 2:  FIND THE FACTS**

**STEP 3:  GET A PLAN**

**STEP 4:  DO THE PROBLEM**

**STEP 5:  DOES YOUR ANSWER MAKE SENSE?**

GO ON

**PROBLEM/QUESTION:**

Kyle feeds the lions in the zoo. It takes him 5 minutes to bring the food out to each lion. He starts feeding the lions at 12:00 noon. At what time will he begin to feed the 3rd lion?

**STEP 1:** **WHAT IS THE QUESTION?**

**STEP 2:** **FIND THE FACTS**

**STEP 3:** **GET A PLAN**

**STEP 4:** **DO THE PROBLEM**

**STEP 5:** **DOES YOUR ANSWER MAKE SENSE?**

STOP

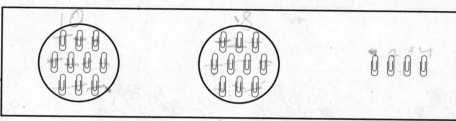

# UNIT SIX
# Math Problem Solving

## Understanding Numeration

**Sample A**

| 24 | 22 | 34 | 44 |
|----|----|----|----|
| ⬤ | ○ | ○ | ○ |

**STOP**

**1**

| 49 | 90 | 94 | 904 |
|----|----|----|-----|
| ○ | ○ | ⬤ | ○ |

**2**

| 427 | 472 | 4,072 | 247 |
|-----|-----|-------|-----|
| ⬤ | ○ | ○ | ○ |

**3**

|  |  |  |  |
|----|----|----|----|
| ○ | ⬤ | ○ | ○ |

**4**

| 302 | 23 | 13 | 32 |
|-----|----|----|----|
| ○ | ○ | ○ | ⬤ |

**5**

**6**

|  |  |  |  |
|----|----|----|----|
| ○ | ○ | ⬤ | ○ |

**STOP**

53

# Using Whole Numbers, Fractions, and Decimals

## Sample A

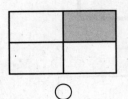 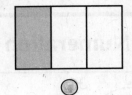 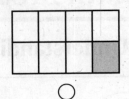 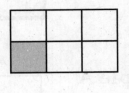

○      ◉      ○      ○

STOP

**1**

◉      ○      ○      ○

**2**

○      ○      ○      ◉

**3**

**8 + 2**   |   2 + 8      8 − 2      10 − 2      10 + 2

◉      ○      ○      ○

**4**

**4 + 3 = 7**

3 + 7 = 10      7 − 2 = 5      4 − 3 = 1      7 − 3 = 4

○      ○      ○      ◉

**5**

**5 + 0 = ☐**   |   10      5      0      1

○      ◉      ○      ○

STOP

54

# Working with Patterns and Relationships

## Sample A

| 75 | 80 | | 90 |
|----|----|----|----|

81 ○    **85** ◉    89 ○    95 ○

STOP

---

## 1

| 3 | 6 | 9 | | 15 |
|---|---|---|----|----|

10 ○    **12** ◉    14 ○    20 ○

---

## 2

**32**  **33**  **34**  **35**

○    ◉    ○    ○

---

## 3

| 18 |
|----|

RECYCLING ○    FOREST ANIMALS ◉    SPACE ○    RIDDLES ○

---

## 4

□ ▲ △ □ ▲ △ □ ▲ △ □

□ ▲ △ □ ▲ △ □ △

◉    ○    ◉    ○

---

## 5

| 57 | 59 | 61 | |

| 60 | 62 | 63 | 64 |

○    ○    ◉    ○

STOP

# Working with Statistics and Probability

## Sample A

| Helpers | | | | | | |
|---|---|---|---|---|---|---|
| Ariana | ★ | ★ | ★ | ★ | | |
| Beata | ★ | | | | | |
| Charles | ★ | ★ | ★ | | | |
| Dante | ★ | ★ | ★ | ★ | ★ | ★ |

Ariana ○    Beata ○    Charles ○    Dante ◉

**STOP**

## 1

| Games Won | |
|---|---|
| Karen | IIII |
| Ling | ₦ |
| Delia | ₦ I |
| Steven | ₦ III |

Karen ○    Ling ◉    Delia ○    Steven ○

## 2

| Reading Chart | | |
|---|---|---|
| Kind of Book | Jerry | Toby |
| Adventure | 3 | 2 |
| Animal | 2 | 5 |
| Poetry | 1 | 1 |

_____

- - - - - - - - - - -

_____

## 3

○    ○    ◉    ○

**STOP**

56

# Working with Geometry

## Sample A

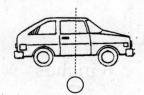  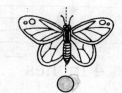 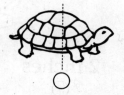

○ ○ ● ○

---

**1**

 |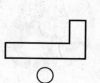

○ ○ ○ ○

● ○ ○ ○

---

**2**

○ ○ ○ ●

---

**3**

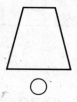  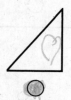 

○ ○ ● ○

---

**4**

 |

○ ○ ● ○

---

**5**

 |

○ ● ○ ○

## Sample A

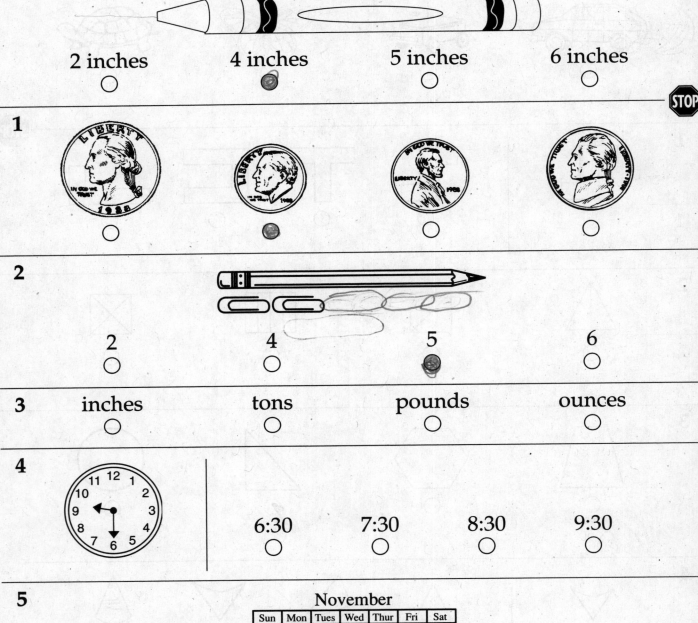

2 inches ○   4 inches ◉   5 inches ○   6 inches ○   **STOP**

**1**   ○   ○   ○   ○

**2**   2 ○   4 ○   5 ◉   6 ○

**3**   inches ○   tons ○   pounds ○   ounces ○

**4**   6:30 ○   7:30 ○   8:30 ○   9:30 ○

**5**

### November

| Sun | Mon | Tues | Wed | Thur | Fri | Sat |
|-----|-----|------|-----|------|-----|-----|
|     |     |      | 1   | 2    | 3   | 4   |
| 5   | 6   | 7    | 8   | 9    | 10  | 11  |
| 12  | 13  | 14   | 15  | 16   | 17  | 18  |
| 19  | 20  | 21   | 22  | 23   | 24  | 25  |
| 26  | 27  | 28   | 29  | 30   |     |     |

**STOP**

# Solving Problems

## Sample A

 ⬛ + 5 = 8          ○ 13 − □ = 8

○ 8 + 5 = [13]          ○ 8 − 5 = □

STOP

**1**

30          23          17          3
○          ○          ○          ○

**2**

20          27          35          40
○          ○          ○          ○

**3**

○ 9 − 4 = □          ○ 5 + 4 = □

○ □ − 4 = 5          ○ 5 − 4 = □

STOP

59

# Understanding Computation

**Sample A**

2          6          8        NH
○          ○          ○        ○

**STOP**

**1**

**10**  **5**

4         15         18        NH
○          ○          ○        ○

**2**

**7**          **12**

19        9         5        NH
○        ○         ○        ○

**3**

**15**        **13**

2        8        38       NH
○        ○        ○       ○

**4**

**5**     **3**

_____

_ _ _ _ _ _ _ _ _ _ _ _ _ _ _ _ _

_____

**GO ON**

**5**

 5      3

_____

- - - - - - - - - - - - - - - - - -

_____

**6**

29      6

| 13 | 23 | 35 | NH |
|----|----|----|----|
| ○ | ○ | ○ | ○ |

**7**

16      8

| 8 | 18 | 24 | NH |
|----|----|----|----|
| ○ | ○ | ○ | ○ |

**8**

45 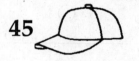     11

| 56 | 54 | 34 | NH |
|----|----|----|----|
| ○ | ○ | ○ | ○ |

**9**

58      42

| 16 | 62 | 100 | NH |
|----|----|----|----|
| ○ | ○ | ○ | ○ |

STOP

# Using Computation

## Sample A

$2 + 5 = \square$

3     6     8     NH
○     ○     ○     ○

**STOP**

**1**     $7 + 7 = \square$

0     12     14     NH
○     ○     ○     ○

**2**     $6 + 4 = \square$

10     5     2     NH
○     ○     ○     ○

**3**

$$\begin{array}{r} 3 \\ 8 \\ + 4 \\ \hline \end{array}$$

13     14     15     NH
○     ○     ○     ○

**4**

$$\begin{array}{r} 65 \\ + 3 \\ \hline \end{array}$$

**5**

$$\begin{array}{r} 30 \\ + 27 \\ \hline \end{array}$$

17     37     57     NH
○     ○     ○     ○

**6**     $8 - 5 = \square$

10     4     3     NH
○     ○     ○     ○

**7**

$$\begin{array}{r} 14 \\ - 5 \\ \hline \end{array}$$

9     10     19     NH
○     ○     ○     ○

**8**

$$\begin{array}{r} 43 \\ - 3 \\ \hline \end{array}$$

**9**

$$\begin{array}{r} 78 \\ - 21 \\ \hline \end{array}$$

99     69     57     NH
○     ○     ○     ○

**10**

$$\begin{array}{r} 460 \\ - 30 \\ \hline \end{array}$$

430     400     490     NH
○     ○     ○     ○

**STOP**

**Sample A**

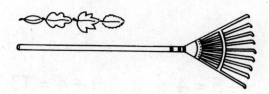

4           6           9           16
○           ○           ○           ○

**STOP**

**Sample B**

28          27          26          25
○           ○           ○           ○

**STOP**

**1**

☐ + 7 = 9

_____

- - - - - - - - - - - - - - - - - - - -

_____

**2**

34, 13          34, 31          43, 13          43, 31
○               ○               ○               ○

**3**

49 ☐ 72          81          73          57          48
                 ○           ○           ○           ○

**4**

| 20 + 5 |          205          75          25          7
                     ○            ○           ○          ○

**GO ON**

**5**

$9 - 4 = 5$

$5 + 9 = 14$ ○   $9 - 5 = 4$ ○   $9 + 4 = 13$ ○   $5 + 2 = 7$ ○

**6**

 ○    ○    ○    ○

**7**

 ○    ○    ○    ○

**8**

○   ○    ○   ○

**9**

| 35 | 40 | 45 |  | 55 |
|----|----|----|----|----|

**10**

 ○    ○    ○    ○   72   73   74   75

**11**

62

 ○    ○    ○    ○

➤ GO ON

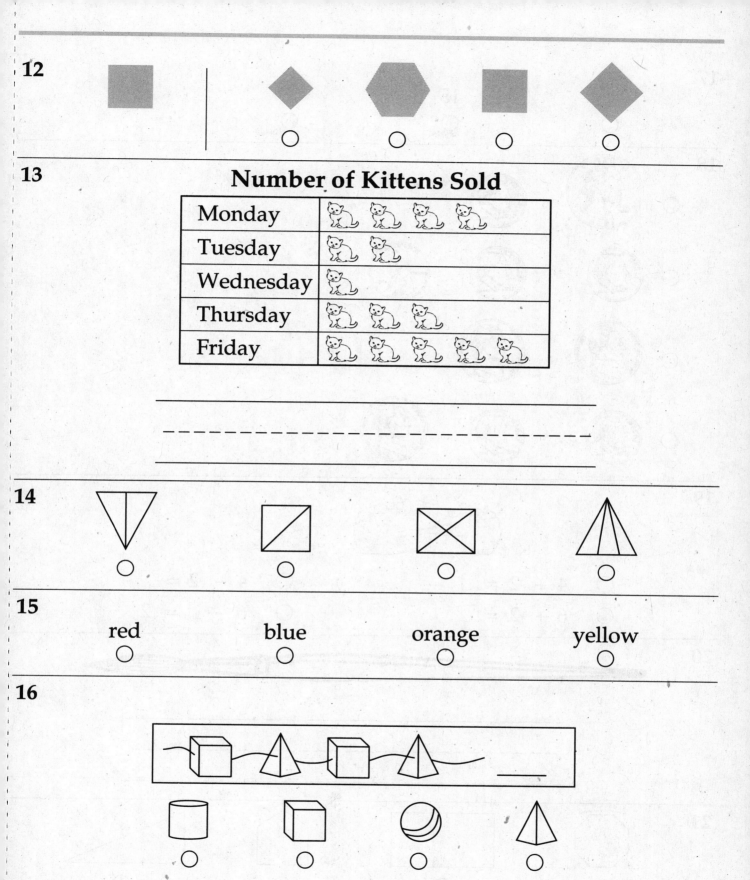

**12**

**13**

**Number of Kittens Sold**

| Monday | |
| --- | --- |
| Tuesday | |
| Wednesday | |
| Thursday | |
| Friday | |

**14**

**15**

red        blue        orange        yellow

**16**

GO ON

**17**

     4             15             19             29

     ○             ○             ○             ○

**18**

○

○

○

○

**19**

○   4 + 2 = ☐          ○   4 − 2 = ☐

○   6 + 2 = ☐          ○   6 − ☐ = 2

**20**

_____

- - - - - - - - - - - - - - - - - - -

_____

**21**

                     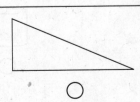

    ○          ○         ○         ○

**STOP**

## Sample C

9 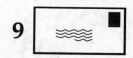   7

    2          3          12         NH
    ○          ○          ○         ○

**STOP**

## Sample D

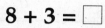

**8 + 3 = ▢**

   11         5          2         NH
   ○          ○          ○         ○

**STOP**

**22**

6    5

**23**

15    4

   29        19         11         NH
   ○          ○          ○         ○

**24**

33    12

   19        39         45         NH
   ○          ○          ○         ○

**GO ON**

**25**

 8    6

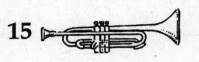

_____

- - - - - - - - - - - - - - - - - - - - - - - - -

_____

---

**26**

15     8

| 7 | 9 | 23 | NH |
|---|---|----|----|
| ○ | ○ | ○  | ○  |

---

**27**

26     3

| 22 | 29 | 32 | NH |
|----|----|----|----|
| ○  | ○  | ○  | ○  |

---

**28**

24     20

| 20 | 14 | 4 | NH |
|----|----|---|----|
| ○  | ○  | ○ | ○  |

---

**29**

57     45

| 12 | 13 | 14 | NH |
|----|----|----|----|
| ○  | ○  | ○  | ○  |

▶ GO ON ▷

68

**30**

$$\begin{array}{r} 9 \\ +\,2 \\ \hline \end{array}$$

5 ○    10 ○    11 ○    NH ○

---

**31**

$$\begin{array}{r} 2 \\ 9 \\ +\,3 \\ \hline \end{array}$$

24 ○    14 ○    12 ○    NH ○

---

**32**

$$\begin{array}{r} 66 \\ +\,3 \\ \hline \end{array}$$

_____

- - - - - - - - - - - - - - - -

_____

---

**33**

$$\begin{array}{r} 38 \\ +\,40 \\ \hline \end{array}$$

48 ○    58 ○    68 ○    NH ○

---

**34**

$$\begin{array}{r} 72 \\ +\,20 \\ \hline \end{array}$$

92 ○    52 ○    50 ○    NH ○

---

**35**

$$5 - 5 = \square$$

5 ○    1 ○    0 ○    NH ○

---

**36**

$$\begin{array}{r} 11 \\ -\,3 \\ \hline \end{array}$$

6 ○    7 ○    8 ○    NH ○

---

**37**

$$\begin{array}{r} 58 \\ -\,6 \\ \hline \end{array}$$

2 ○    22 ○    52 ○    NH ○

---

**38**

$$\begin{array}{r} 80 \\ -\,20 \\ \hline \end{array}$$

_____

- - - - - - - - - - - - - - - -

_____

---

**39**

$$\begin{array}{r} 549 \\ -\,45 \\ \hline \end{array}$$

594 ○    584 ○    504 ○    NH ○

**STOP**

## Listening for Word Meanings

**Sample A**
- ○ flute
- ⊘ fiddle
- ○ violet

**STOP**

**1**
- ○ help
- ○ heal
- ⊖ hurt

**2**
- ○ hide it
- ○ find it
- ○ bury it

**3**
- ○ limp
- ○ bunch
- ○ shade

**4**
- ○ save
- ○ wash
- ○ feed

**5**
- ○ get lighter
- ○ get darker
- ○ get smaller

**6**
- ○ box
- ○ present
- ○ cake

**7**
- ○ wait
- ○ sleep
- ○ hurry

**8**
- ○ clap
- ○ mark
- ⊘ point

**9**
- ○ creek
- ○ sea
- ○ pond

**10**
- ○ replace it
- ⊘ fix it
- ○ return it

**11**
- ○ over
- ○ above
- ⊘ under

**12**
- ○ yell
- ○ laugh
- ⊘ cry

**STOP**

# Choosing Picture Answers

**Sample A**

◯     ◯     ◯

**STOP**

**1**

◯     ◯     ◯

**2**

◯     ◯     ◯

**3**

◯     ◯     ◯

**4**

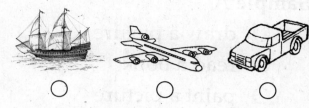

◯     ◯     ◯

**5**

◯     ◯     ◯

**6**

◯     ◯     ◯

**7**

◯     ◯     ◯

**STOP**

71

# Building Listening Skills

**Sample A**
- ○ draw a picture
- ○ read a book
- ○ paint a picture

**STOP**

**1**
- ○ today
- ○ seven days ago
- ○ two weeks ago

**2**
- ○ smile
- ○ talk
- ○ eat

**3**
- ○ It was raining.
- ○ There was a parade.
- ○ They were on their way to Africa.

**4**
- ○ elephants
- ○ ferrets
- ○ giraffes

**5**
- ○ as small as bees
- ○ as small as teacups
- ○ as small as chickens

**6**
- ○ from the things they left behind
- ○ from the people who were living then
- ○ from animals today

**7**
- ○ biscuits
- ○ French toast
- ○ cereal

**8**
- ○ add the bread
- ○ put it on the stove
- ○ stir in some butter

**9**
- ○ Courtney
- ○ Courtney's mom
- ○ Courtney's whole family

**STOP**

# Unit 7 Test

## Sample A

- ○ shout
- ○ laugh
- ○ whisper

**STOP**

1  ○ shed
   ○ boat
   ○ small house

2  ○ calm down
   ○ leave
   ○ get ready

3  ○ insect
   ○ igloo
   ○ pet

4  ○ hit
   ○ smooth
   ○ clean

5  ○ illness
   ○ trip
   ○ excuse

6  ○ present
   ○ late
   ○ early

7  ○ tomorrow
   ○ tonight
   ○ yesterday

8  ○ nice
   ○ rude
   ○ poor

9  ○ not common
   ○ square
   ○ normal

10 ○ not afraid
   ○ not angry
   ○ not smart

11 ○ go away
   ○ be seen
   ○ get faster

12 ○ ocean
   ○ desert
   ○ forest

**STOP**

## Sample B

    ○       ○       ○

**STOP**

---

**13**

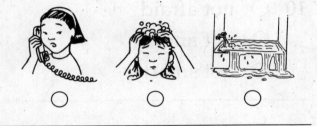

    ○       ○       ○

---

**14**

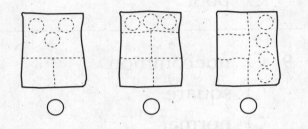

    ○       ○       ○

---

**15**

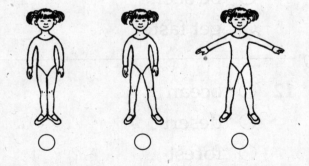

    ○       ○       ○

---

**16**

    ○       ○       ○

---

**17**

    ○       ○       ○

---

**18**

    ○       ○       ○

---

**19**

    ○       ○       ○

---

**20**

    ○       ○       ○

---

**21**

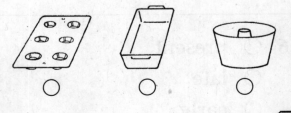

    ○       ○       ○

**STOP**

**Sample C**
- ○ store
- ○ museum
- ○ park

———————————— **STOP**

**22**
- ○ the kite can fly
- ○ the kite won't blow away
- ○ you can decorate the kite

**23**
- ○ attach some string
- ○ insert wooden pieces
- ○ paint the kite

**24**
- ○ sweeping the store
- ○ taking out the trash
- ○ turning out all the lights

**25**
- ○ doing his homework
- ○ taking out the trash
- ○ turning out all the lights

**26**
- ○ taking a shower
- ○ catching rainwater
- ○ taking a bath

**27**
- ○ soap up your hands
- ○ rinse
- ○ take a bath

**28**
- ○ his frog
- ○ his snake
- ○ his homework

**29**
- ○ surprised
- ○ tired
- ○ sad

**30**
- ○ practicing a play
- ○ running a race
- ○ doing a science experiment

**31**
- ○ Michiko
- ○ Jenna
- ○ Jamal

**32**
- ○ sleeping bags
- ○ radio
- ○ flashlights

**33**
- ○ "How to Go Camping"
- ○ "The Díaz Family's Problem"
- ○ "Fun with Flashlights"

**STOP**

# Language

## Listening to Stories

### Sample A

 ○     ○     ○

STOP

**1**   ○     ○     ○

**2**   ○     ●    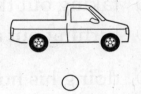 ○

**3**   ○     ○     ○

**4**   ○     ○     ○

STOP

# Prewriting, Composing, and Editing

**Sample A**

**Julie's Trip to Mexico**

Julie's Journal

| Swimming in the ocean | Shopping in the market at home | Games we play on the ship |
|---|---|---|
| ○ | ◉ | ○ |

**STOP**

**Sample B**

> Shopping was fun.
> Mother <u>buyed</u> me a hat.

| bought | buy | Correct the way it is. |
|---|---|---|
| ○ | ○ | ○ |

**STOP**

**Sample C**

> We swam in the water.
> And played in the waves.
> We made sand castles.

- ○  We swam in the water.
- ◉  And played in the waves.
- ○  We made sand castles.

**STOP**

## Larry's Horse

1
- ○ to tell how to teach a horse tricks
- ○ to tell why he loves horses
- ◉ to tell a story about his pet

2
| kiss | tricks | hand |
|:----:|:------:|:----:|
| ○ | ○ |  |

### My Smart Horse

My horse can do many tricks.
He lifts his leg to my hand shake.
He gives me a kiss with his nose.
My horse can also play hiding games.

3
- ○ He lifts his leg to hand shake my.
- ◉ He lifts his leg to shake my hand.
- ○ Correct the way it is.

4
- ○ My horse is brown and white.
- ○ I like to see my horse run.
- ○ My horse comes when he sees me.

GO ON

> I <u>gived</u> my horse a treat after each trick.
> (1)
>
> He <u>likes</u> carrots best.
> (2)
>
> If I forget his treat, he shakes his head.

**5**   gave ○     give ○     Correct the way it is. ○

**6**   like ○     liked ○     Correct the way it is. ○

*Going Places*

**7**   1 ○     2 ○     3 ○

**8**   21 ○     38 ○     50 ○

▶ GO ON ▶

79

## Getting Around in the City

Many people drive cars.
In large cities.
Some people ride in taxis.
Most people ride the bus.

**9**  ○ Many people drive cars.
     ○ In large cities.
     ○ Some people ride in taxis.

**10** ○ A few people might walk to work.
     ○ People work in a city.
     ○ The city is noisy.

We lives in the city.
(1)

My father rides a bus to work.
(2)

It is too far for him to walk.

**11**  We is living        We live        Correct the way it is.
         ○                  ○                  ○

**12**  My Father          my father      Correct the way it is.
         ○                  ○                  ○

GO ON

80

## A Surprise for Father

**13**
- ○ bake her father a cake
- ○ make a list of things she does with her father
- ○ read a book of poems

**14**
- ○ a birthday party
- ○ a present Rena will give her father
- ○ things Rena likes to do with her father

My Family

Together we have fun.
We laugh and we run.
We fish in the lake.
And Mother likes to bake.
Sometimes we go on hikes.

**15**
- ○ Together we have fun.
- ○ We fish in the lake.
- ○ And Mother likes to bake.

**16**
- ○ And then we ride our bikes.
- ○ I am happy.
- ○ You are fun.

GO ON

Dear Father,
(1)

Are you having a fun <u>birthday</u>
                  (2)

<u>I wanted</u> to make it special.
(3)

I love you.

Your daughter,
Rena

---

**17**    Dear father,       dear Father,       Correct the way it is.
           ○                ○              ○

---

**18**      birthday?          birthday.         birthday!
           ○                ○              ○

---

**19**      I wants          I wanting       Correct the way it is.
           ○                ○              ○

STOP

# Finding Misspelled Words

**Sample A**
- ○ wint
- ○ along
- ○ ride

🛑 STOP

1
- ○ you
- ○ see
- ○ bakt

2
- ○ wus
- ○ eating
- ○ apple

3
- ○ walkt
- ○ store
- ○ himself

4
- ○ two
- ○ babies
- ○ playd

5
- ○ had
- ○ party
- ○ skool

6
- ○ Pleaze
- ○ pass
- ○ milk

7
- ○ can
- ○ cros
- ○ street

8
- ○ boyes
- ○ joined
- ○ team

9
- ○ frog
- ○ gren
- ○ grass

10
- ○ turn
- ○ wash
- ○ dishs

11
- ○ pickd
- ○ these
- ○ flowers

🛑 STOP

# Unit 8 Test

**Sample A**

      ○            ●            ○

**STOP**

**1**

      ○            ○            ●

**2**

      ○            ○            ○

**3**

  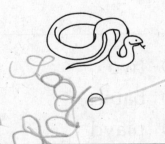

      ●            ○            ○

**4**

      ○            ○            ○

**STOP**

84

**Sample B**

*Takshi's Friend*

To my Pen Pal

| What Takshi looks like | Why Takshi wants a pen pal | Games Takshi likes to play |
|:---:|:---:|:---:|
| ○ | ○ | ◉ |

**Sample C**

Dear Peter,

I want to tell you about me.
I am in the first grade.
I like to play baseball.
Every day after school.

○ I am in the first grade.
○ I like to play baseball.
◉ Every day after school.

**Sample D**

Will you <u>writing</u> soon?
I want to know more about you.
Your friend,
Takshi

write          writes          Correct the way it is.
○                ○                ○

## Pat's Science Project

**5**
- ⊖ list ways seeds move
- ○ plant some seeds
- ○ glue seeds to paper

**6**
- ○ buy seeds from a store
- ⊖ find a library book about seeds
- ○ go to a park

### Animals Help Move Seeds

Some animals help move seeds.
Birds pick up seeds to eat.
They may <u>dropping</u> the seeds as they fly.
I have a new dog.
The seeds grow where they fall on the ground.

GO ON

**7**

- ○ drops
- ⊖ drop
- ○ Correct the way it is.

**8**

- ○ Some animals help move seeds.
- ○ Birds pick up seeds to eat.
- ⊖ I have a new dog.

Some seeds stick to the fur of animals.
They <u>dont</u> fall off easily.
The ends of the seeds are turned up.

**9**

- ⊘ don't
- ○ do'nt
- ○ Correct the way it is.

**10**

- ○ The seed ends look sharp and look like a fishhook.
- ○ The seed ends look sharp and like a fishhook.
- ⊘ The seed ends look like a sharp fishhook.

**11**

| stick | seeds | sharp |
|:---:|:---:|:---:|
| ○ | ○ | ○ |

▶GO ON▶

## Mr. Lee's New Car

$599
PER MONTH

**12**
- ○ talk to a car salesperson
- ○ drive a car
- ○ look under a car

**13**

a red car ○          a safe car ○          wash the car ○

▶ GO ON

## Car Safety

The car should be very safe. It needs seat belts in the front and the back. It must have new tires. The horn should honk. Very loudly for people to hear.

**14**
- ○ The car will have two doors.
- ○ I want a car I saw at the store.
- ○ It should be a new car.

**15**
- ○ The car should be very safe.
- ○ It must have new tires.
- ○ Very loudly for people to hear.

GO ON

Car for Sale

I <u>have</u> a car for sale.
   **(1)**
It is in very good shape.
I need to sell it before <u>Thursday, june 28.</u>
                              **(2)**

**16**    had            has            Correct the way it is.
          ○              ○              ○

**17**    ○  thursday, june 28.
          ○  Thursday, June 28.
          ○  Correct the way it is.

**18**    ○  Please call to find out more.
          ○  The car is sold.
          ○  I want to buy a blue car.

(STOP)

**Sample E**
- ○ play
- ○ overe
- ○ four

**STOP**

**19**
- ○ prety
- ○ pink
- ○ present

**20**
- ○ told
- ○ funny
- ○ storie

**21**
- ○ This
- ○ ende
- ○ line

**22**
- ○ boys
- ○ splashd
- ○ water

**23**
- ○ bought
- ○ two
- ○ brushs

**24**
- ○ mean
- ○ what
- ○ sed

**25**
- ○ pond
- ○ filld
- ○ fish

**26**
- ○ fase
- ○ has
- ○ dirt

**27**
- ○ put
- ○ toyes
- ○ room

**28**
- ○ Mother
- ○ parkt
- ○ close

**29**
- ○ livz
- ○ under
- ○ rock

**STOP**

## Reading Comprehension

**Sample A**

You can climb it.
It is made of wood.

○   ○   ○

**4** It is found in space.
It can fly.

○   ○   ○

---

**1** I have four legs.
I cannot walk or run.

○   ○   ○

**5** I am big.
I have fur.

○   ○   ○

---

**2** I have stripes.
I can growl.

○   ○   ○

**6** It has strings.
It makes music.

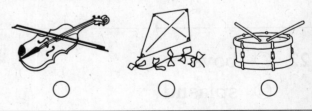

○   ○   ○

---

**3** You can rock on it.
It is a toy.

○   ○   ○

**7** It can float.
It can swim.

○   ○   ○

---

 You have 40 minutes to complete this test.

**Sample**

**B  Gino is riding his big brother's**

tricycle        bicycle        wagon
 ○              ○              ○

**C  Gino splashed water on Ms. Zamora's**

dress        hat        car
 ○          ○          ○

**STOP**

**8  Aunt Abby is feeding her**

puppy        baby        self
 ○            ○          ○

**9  The baby is drinking from a**

cup        bottle        straw
 ○          ○            ○

**10  The children are in a**

classroom        store        mall
 ○                ○            ○

**11  They listen to**

a farmer        an artist        a teacher
 ○                ○                ○

**STOP**

**12  Eileen is holding a**

stick        fishing pole        broom
 ○              ○                ○

**13  She caught a**

cold        rabbit        fish
 ○          ○            ○

**14  Eileen is**

jumping        frowning        smiling
 ○                ○                ○

**STOP**

93

**Sample D
Learning from Dad**

Toni and her dad made little holes in the ground. They put a seed in each hole. Then they covered the seeds. Toni poured water on the ground. Then she said, "Now we will have good things to eat."

**What were Toni and her dad doing?**

○ eating seeds

○ watering flowers

○ planting a garden

**Maria's Party**

Maria is having a party. Her father made a cake, and her mother blew up balloons. Maria's friends are coming and bringing gifts for Maria. Maria will blow out the candles on the cake. Then everyone will have cake and milk.

**15  How did Maria's mom help with the party?**

○ She made a cake.

◑ She blew up balloons.

○ She blew out the candles.

**16  What will Maria's friends bring with them?**

○ cake

○ balloons

○ gifts

**17  Where are the candles?**

○ on the gifts

◑ on the cake

○ on the table

**18  What kind of party is Maria probably having?**

◑ a birthday party

○ a swimming party

○ a New Year's party

GO ON

## Interesting Insects

Caterpillars and butterflies are interesting insects. They live in many places in the world. They live in cool places. They live in hot places.

Caterpillars are born in the early spring. They eat for many months. Then they become butterflies.

There are many kinds of butterflies. Some butterflies live only for a few weeks. Other butterflies live for several months. Some butterflies are brown and green. They can hide in the trees. Other butterflies have bright colors. All these butterflies help make a colorful world.

**19  Where do caterpillars and butterflies live?**

○  only in hot places

○  only in cold places

○  in many places in the world

**20  From this story you know that**

○  caterpillars eat very little.

○  all butterflies live a long time.

○  there are many different kinds of butterflies.

**21  When do caterpillars become butterflies?**

○  in early spring

○  after eating for many months

○  after several years

**22  Why can some butterflies hide in trees?**

○  Their colors are the same as the colors of a tree.

○  They have very bright colors.

○  They are very small.

▶ GO ON ▶

## Ranch Vacation

Helen and Jim went to stay at a dude ranch with their families. They saw this sign.

### Daily Events

| | |
|---|---|
| 8:00 A.M. | Breakfast Cookout |
| 10:00 A.M. | Trail Ride |
| Noon | Chuckwagon Lunch |
| 2:00 P.M. | Cowboy Show |
| 4:00 P.M. | Hay Ride |
| 6:00 P.M. | Dinner and Barn Dance |

**23** **What does the sign say?**

- ○ how much things cost at the dude ranch
- ○ how to get to the dude ranch
- ○ things to do at the dude ranch

**24** **What will Helen and Jim probably go to just before the Chuckwagon Lunch?**

- ○ Hay Ride
- ○ Trail Ride
- ○ Cowboy Show

**25** **What time does the Cowboy Show start?**

_____

_ _ _ _ _ _ _ _ _ _ _ _ _ _ _

**26** **What is the last event of the day?**

- ○ Dinner and Barn Dance
- ○ Hay Ride
- ○ Cowboy Show

▶GO ON▶

# A Day of Fun

Kim went to the circus. She saw many things. There were three dancing bears. One of them wore a skirt. She also saw an elephant walk on its back legs.

Kim saw a tall clown in a little car. She laughed when the clown got stuck.

Kim looked up to watch people walking on wires. She sat very still. She was afraid they would fall. Kim wants to visit the circus again.

**27  This story tells about**
- ○  Kim's dog.
- ○  how to be a clown.
- ○  a trip to the circus.

**28  On how many legs did the elephant walk?**

_____

_____2_____

**29  Why did Kim laugh?**
- ○  She thought the clown was funny.
- ○  She thought the people on wires were funny.
- ○  She told a joke.

**30  You can tell that Kim**
- ○  didn't like the circus.
- ○  wants to go to the zoo.
- ○  enjoyed the circus.

>GO ON▶

## Life on the Farm

Lia lives on a farm. She helps her mother milk the cows. She helps her father gather the chicken eggs. Lia has fun with the farm animals. She gives each one a name. Sometimes the baby goats follow her around. They follow her to the pond where she swims. While she splashes, they eat grass and watch. Lia likes living on a farm. She wants to be a farmer when she grows up.

**31  This story is about**

- ○ growing a garden.
- ○ living in a city.
- ◉ living on a farm.

**32  Lia must be good at**

- ○ singing.
- ◉ swimming.
- ○ painting.

**33  What does Lia give each animal?**

A Name

**34  You can tell that Lia**

- ○ enjoys living on the farm.
- ○ does not like living on the farm.
- ○ does not like hard work.

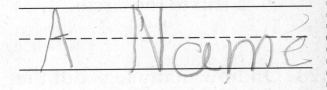

GO ON

## Juan's Wish

Juan is from Mexico. It is very warm there. It never snows where he lives. Juan has cousins in Maine. It is cold there in the winter. It snows there every year. His cousins like to play in the snow. They send pictures of the snow to Juan. He has always wanted to see the snow for himself. Last winter Juan's aunt and uncle invited him to Maine. He was very excited! He knew he would play in the snow with his cousins. Before the trip, Juan got his first winter coat, hat, and gloves. Still, he felt cold when he went outside. His aunt told him that it would snow soon. He wanted to build a snowman. He did not want to go back to Mexico until he saw snow. "Surprise!" said his aunt one morning a few days later. Juan ran outside.

**35** **What did Juan want more than anything?**

- ◉ to see snow
- ○ to play on a beach
- ○ a new winter coat

**36** **Who invited Juan to Maine?**

- ○ his friend
- ◉ his aunt and uncle
- ○ his parents

**37** **Juan wanted to build a**

Snowman

**38** **Why did Juan's aunt say, "Surprise!"**

- ○ Juan had to go home.
- ◉ It had snowed the night before.
- ○ Someone came to visit.

## Vocabulary and Word Study Skills

**Sample**

| | | | | | | |
|---|---|---|---|---|---|---|
| **A** | boot ○ | boat ○ | plane ○ | **7** | play ○ | study ○ | sleep ○ |
| **B** | above ○ | beyond ○ | below ○ | **8** | football ○ | baseball ○ | swimming ○ |
| **C** | sea ○ | sand ○ | shore ○ | **9** | library ○ | part ○ | park ○ |

**STOP**

| | | | | | | |
|---|---|---|---|---|---|---|
| **1** | locks ○ | build ○ | lift ○ | **10** | plant ○ | under ○ | jumping ○ |
| **2** | books ○ | lands ○ | blocks ○ | **11** | ribbon ○ | rope ○ | place ○ |
| **3** | careful ○ | sad ○ | sleepy ○ | **12** | rode ○ | play ○ | running ○ |

| | | | | | | |
|---|---|---|---|---|---|---|
| **4** | feast ○ | army ○ | feed ○ | **13** | cart ○ | car ○ | soup ○ |
| **5** | goats ○ | ghost ○ | shoes ○ | **14** | wash ○ | wagon ○ | shine ○ |
| **6** | far ○ | toast ○ | farm ○ | **15** | not ○ | soap ○ | mop ○ |

**STOP**

You have 50 minutes to complete this test.

**Sample D**
- ○ lovely
- ○ ladybug
- ○ magic

**STOP**

**16**
- ○ player
- ○ pillow
- ○ afternoon

**17**
- ○ hardness
- ○ quickly
- ○ footsteps

**18**
- ○ haircut
- ○ sweeping
- ○ feather

**19**
- ○ ponytail
- ○ shining
- ○ larger

**20**
- ○ narrow
- ○ rooftop
- ○ saucer

**21**
- ○ super
- ○ sailboat
- ○ loudly

**22**
- ○ picnic
- ○ baseball
- ○ above

**23**
- ○ pencil
- ○ daytime
- ○ buying

**24**
- ○ names
- ○ basket
- ○ beehive

**25**
- ○ doorbell
- ○ harmful
- ○ penny

**26**
- ○ cupcake
- ○ gum
- ○ cracked

**STOP**

**Sample E**

- ○ open
- ○ openly
- ○ opening

(STOP)

**27**
- ○ weeks
- ○ weekly
- ○ weekend

**28**
- ○ peek
- ○ peeking
- ○ peeks

**29**
- ○ teaching
- ○ teach
- ○ teaches

**30**
- ○ mask
- ○ masks
- ○ masked

**31**
- ○ buyer
- ○ buys
- ○ buying

(STOP)

**Sample F**

- ○ he'll
- ○ he's
- ○ he'd

(STOP)

**32**
- ○ she'll
- ○ she's
- ○ she'd

**33**
- ○ couldn't
- ○ isn't
- ○ can't

**34**
- ○ wasn't
- ○ weren't
- ○ won't

**35**
- ○ we'll
- ○ we've
- ○ we'd

**36**
- ○ I'm
- ○ I'd
- ○ I've

(STOP)

**Sample G**

**glad**

| glue | gum | green |
|:---:|:---:|:---:|
| ○ | ○ | ○ |

STOP

**37 lunch**

| soup | true | tummy |
|:---:|:---:|:---:|
| ○ | ○ | ○ |

**38 bat**

| game | ladder | hay |
|:---:|:---:|:---:|
| ○ | ○ | ○ |

**39 hiss**

| hire | dive | will |
|:---:|:---:|:---:|
| ○ | ○ | ○ |

**40 state**

| spring | shovel | first |
|:---:|:---:|:---:|
| ○ | ○ | ○ |

**41 circle**

| chair | center | shoe |
|:---:|:---:|:---:|
| ○ | ○ | ○ |

**42 those**

| cart | rose | there |
|:---:|:---:|:---:|
| ○ | ○ | ○ |

**43 clear**

| crowd | close | coal |
|:---:|:---:|:---:|
| ○ | ○ | ○ |

**44 door**

| wore | stop | rope |
|:---:|:---:|:---:|
| ○ | ○ | ○ |

**45 curl**

| corn | shirt | thing |
|:---:|:---:|:---:|
| ○ | ○ | ○ |

**46 mouse**

| pony | bunny | lamb |
|:---:|:---:|:---:|
| ○ | ○ | ○ |

**47 give**

| car | wall | forget |
|:---:|:---:|:---:|
| ○ | ○ | ○ |

**48 boat**

| pot | open | moon |
|:---:|:---:|:---:|
| ○ | ○ | ○ |

STOP

## Sample H

◯    ◯    ◯

**STOP**

### 49

◯    ◯    ◯

### 50

type    time    think
◯    ◯    ◯

### 51

sink    hurt    push
◯    ◯    ◯

### 52

rabbit    narrow    bottle
◯    ◯    ◯

### 53

◯    ◯    ◯

### 54

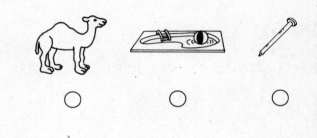

◯    ◯    ◯

### 55

blood    wood    food
◯    ◯    ◯

### 56

please    choose    nest
◯    ◯    ◯

▶ GO ON ▶

**57 hard**

    ed          ing          ly

    ○          ○          ○

**58 bring**

    ing          ly          ed

    ○          ○          ○

**59 catch**

    ly          er          ness

    ○          ○          ○

**60 new**

    est          ing          ed

    ○          ○          ○

**61 miss**

    est          ly          ed

    ○          ○          ○

**62 good**

    est          ness          er

    ○          ○          ○

**STOP**

## Part 1: Math Problem Solving

**Sample A**

○      ○      ○      ○      **STOP**

**Sample B**

| 32 | 23 | 21 | 3 |
|----|----|----|---|
| ○  | ○  | ○  | ○ |

**STOP**

**1**

| 315 | 350 | 3015 | 153 |
|-----|-----|------|-----|
| ○   | ○   | ○    | ○   |

**2**

○          ○          ○          ○

**3**

| 6 | 106 | 56 | 66 |
|---|-----|----|----|
| ○ | ○   | ○  | ○  |

**4**

   ○       ○    ○          ○

**GO ON**

 You have 40 minutes to complete this test.

**5**

| 50 + 8 | 85 ◯ | 508 ◯ | 58 ◯ | 580 ◯ |

**6**

42

| 32 ◯ | 52 ◯ | 41 ◯ | 24 ◯ |

**7**

5 + 1 = 6

| 6 + 5 = 11 ◯ | 6 − 5 = 1 ◯ | 5 − 1 = 4 ◯ | 6 + 1 = 7 ◯ |

**8**

8 + 0 = ☐

_____

- - - - - - - - - - - - - - - - - -

_____

**9**

45 ☐ 69

| 81 ◯ | 38 ◯ | 73 ◯ | 52 ◯ |

**10**

| 71, 72 ◯ | 27, 17 ◯ | 71, 17 ◯ | 71, 67 ◯ |

▶GO ON▶

**11**

$3 + 4$ | $4 - 3$     $7 + 3$     $7 - 4$     $4 + 3$
                      ○         ○         ○         ○

**12**

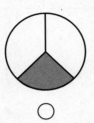     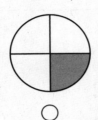     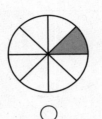    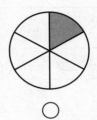

○        ○        ○        ○

**13**

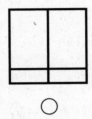     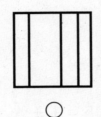     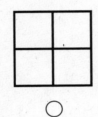    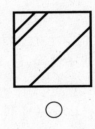

○        ○        ○        ○

**14**

○        ○        ○        ○

**15**

| 30 | 35 | | 45 |
|----|----|----|----|

▶GO ON

**16**

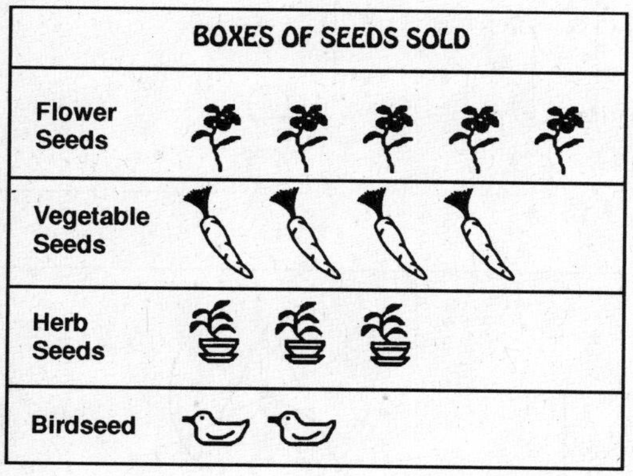
BOXES OF SEEDS SOLD
Flower Seeds
Vegetable Seeds
Herb Seeds
Birdseed

2 ○ 3 ○ 4 ○ 5 ○

**17**

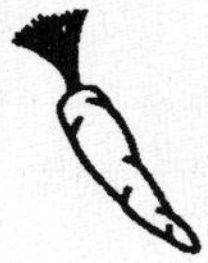 ○
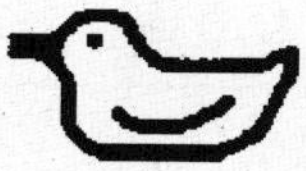 ○
 ○
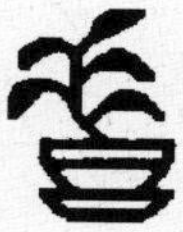 ○

**18**

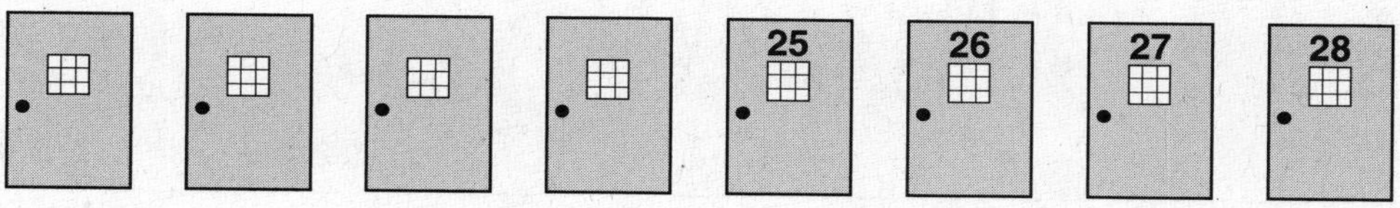
25
26
27
28

○ ○ ○ ○

**19**

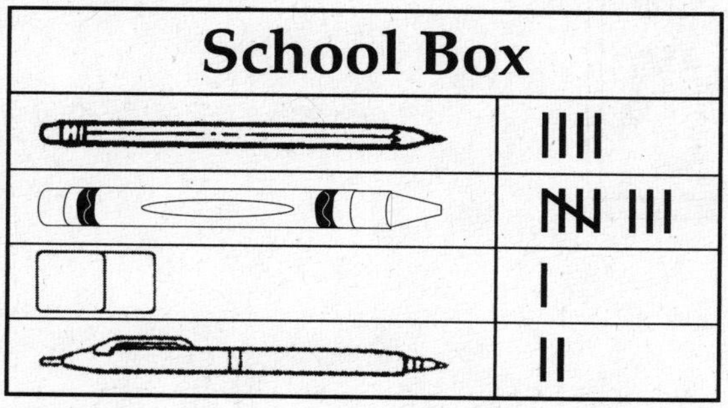
School Box

______________________________

**20**

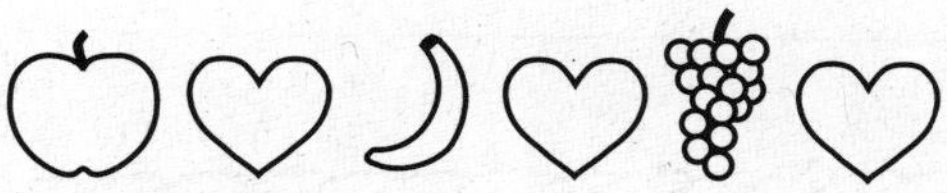

 ○
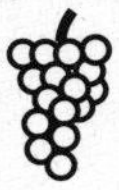 ○
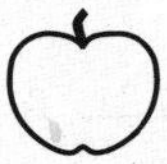 ○
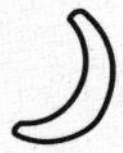 ○

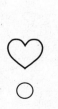

GO ON

**21**

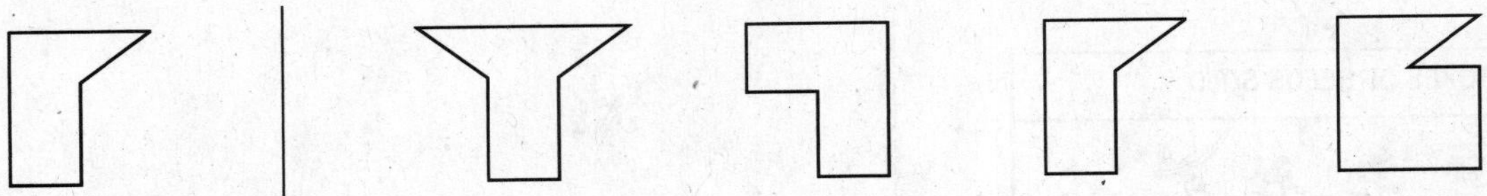

○        ○        ○        ○

**22**

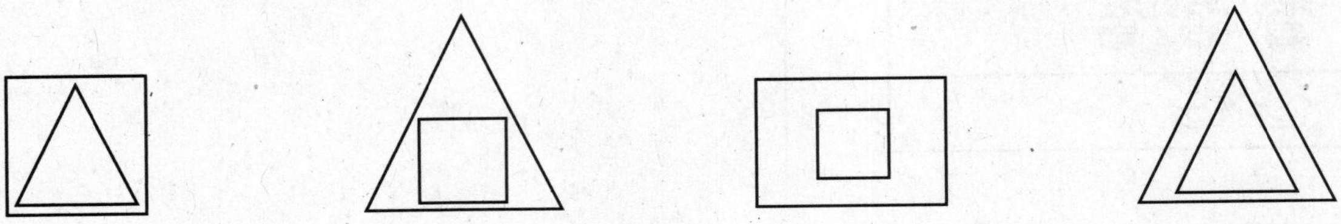

○        ○        ○        ○

**23**

○        ○        ○        ○

**24**

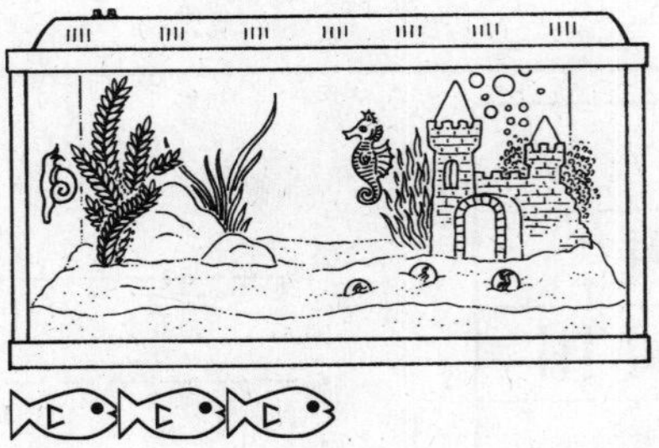

9          2          4          6
○          ○          ○          ○

**25**

GO ON ▶

**26**

○

○

○

○

---

**27**

| miles | inches | cups | gallons |
|:---:|:---:|:---:|:---:|
| ○ | ○ | ○ | ○ |

---

**28**

| 9:30 | 3:30 | 4:30 | 4:00 |
|:---:|:---:|:---:|:---:|
| ○ | ○ | ○ | ○ |

---

▶GO ON▶

**29**

      15                  42                 54                 65
      ○                  ○                 ○                 ○

---

**30**

○   5 − □ = 2
○   5 − 2 = □
○   2 + 2 = □
○   5 + 2 = □

---

**31**

      28                  18                 14                 11
      ○                  ○                 ○                 ○

---

**32**

## October

| Sun | Mon | Tues | Wed | Thur | Fri | Sat |
|-----|-----|------|-----|------|-----|-----|
|  |  |  | 1 | 2 | 3 | 4 |
| 5 | 6 | 7 | 8 | 9 | 10 | 11 |
| 12 | 13 | 14 | 15 | 16 | 17 | 18 |
| 19 | 20 | 21 | 22 | 23 | 24 | 25 |
| 26 | 27 | 28 | 29 | 30 | 31 |  |

STOP

## Sample C

5     8

14  ○    13  ○    12  ○    NH ○

**STOP**

## Sample D

$$9 + 2 = \square$$

_____

- - - - - - - - - - -

_____

**STOP**

**1**

7     3

4 ○    10 ○    13 ○    NH ○

**2**

20     15

5 ○    25 ○    35 ○    NH ○

**GO ON**

You have 30 minutes to complete this test.

**3**

 7  4

_____

- - - - - - - - - - - - - - - - - -

_____

**4**

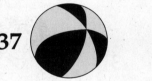 16  6

22      10     8     NH
○      ○      ○      ○

**5**

 37   4

41     3     33     NH
○      ○      ○      ○

**6**

 50   30

20     40     80     NH
○      ○      ○      ○

▶ GO ON

**7**    4 + 3 = ☐

1      6      8     NH
○      ○      ○     ○

---

**8**
$$\begin{array}{r} 5 \\ + 5 \\ \hline \end{array}$$

_____

- - - - - - - - - - - - - - - -

_____

---

**9**
$$\begin{array}{r} 9 \\ + 6 \\ \hline \end{array}$$

16    15    3    NH
○     ○     ○    ○

---

**10**
$$\begin{array}{r} 4 \\ 2 \\ + 3 \\ \hline \end{array}$$

8     7     6    NH
○     ○     ○    ○

---

**11**
$$\begin{array}{r} 53 \\ + 2 \\ \hline \end{array}$$

55    59    61   NH
○     ○     ○    ○

---

**12**
$$\begin{array}{r} 83 \\ + 6 \\ \hline \end{array}$$

99    89    77   NH
○     ○     ○    ○

---

**13**
$$\begin{array}{r} 62 \\ + 10 \\ \hline \end{array}$$

82    80    72   NH
○     ○     ○    ○

---

**14**
$$\begin{array}{r} 27 \\ + 21 \\ \hline \end{array}$$

48    46    6    NH
○     ○     ○    ○

---

**15**
$$\begin{array}{r} 9 \\ 4 \\ + 5 \\ \hline \end{array}$$

16    17    18   NH
○     ○     ○    ○

---

**16**
$$\begin{array}{r} 66 \\ + 22 \\ \hline \end{array}$$

_____

- - - - - - - - - - - - - - - -

_____

▶GO ON

**17**  $8 - 7 = \square$

0      1     15     NH
○     ○     ○     ○

**18**  $13 - 6 = \square$

7     8     28     NH
○     ○     ○     ○

**19**
$$\begin{array}{r} 14 \\ -7 \\ \hline \end{array}$$

7     8     21     NH
○     ○     ○     ○

**20**
$$\begin{array}{r} 45 \\ -4 \\ \hline \end{array}$$

**21**
$$\begin{array}{r} 98 \\ -3 \\ \hline \end{array}$$

96     94     65     NH
○     ○     ○     ○

**22**
$$\begin{array}{r} 62 \\ -51 \\ \hline \end{array}$$

113     13     11     NH
○     ○     ○     ○

**23**
$$\begin{array}{r} 70 \\ -20 \\ \hline \end{array}$$

**24**  $25 - 6 = \square$

31     19     18     NH
○     ○     ○     ○

**25**
$$\begin{array}{r} 17 \\ -8 \\ \hline \end{array}$$

25     19     9     NH
○     ○     ○     ○

**26**
$$\begin{array}{r} 328 \\ -18 \\ \hline \end{array}$$

300     310     318     NH
○     ○     ○     ○

STOP

UNIT TWELVE

# Practice Test 4

## Listening

**Sample A**

○ forehead
○ brain
○ heart

STOP

**1** ○ surprise
○ upset
○ scare

**2** ○ brave
○ easy
○ quickly

**3** ○ happy
○ worried
○ funny

**4** ○ bring down
○ lift
○ fold

**5** ○ lazy
○ sick
○ absent

**6** ○ front
○ rear
○ middle

**7** ○ take care of
○ leave
○ talk about

**8** ○ song
○ book
○ drawing

**9** ○ change
○ tear
○ count

**10** ○ excited
○ angry
○ silly

**11** ○ an avenue
○ a corner
○ a road

**12** ○ dash
○ wander
○ slide

STOP

You have 25 minutes to complete this test.

# Sample B

STOP

13

14

15

16

17

18

19

20

21

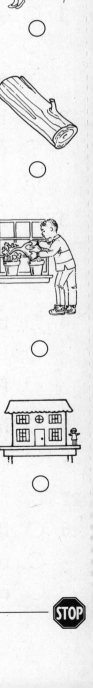

STOP

118

**Sample C**
- ○ a flag
- ○ an umbrella
- ○ a sandwich

STOP

22
- ○ discuss books
- ○ play softball
- ○ put on puppet plays

23
- ○ sleep
- ○ cook
- ○ study

24
- ○ California
- ○ Hawaii
- ○ Alaska

25
- ○ sail on a boat
- ○ ride in a car
- ○ fly in a plane

26
- ○ come to visit
- ○ are leaving
- ○ have a birthday

27
- ○ "Rolanda and Her Aunts"
- ○ "Celebrations in Mexico"
- ○ "Rolanda's Trips to Mexico"

28
- ○ became tired
- ○ stumbled and fell
- ○ ran off to play

29
- ○ sand
- ○ snow
- ○ dirt

30
- ○ hat
- ○ nose
- ○ arms

31
- ○ afraid
- ○ proud
- ○ angry

32
- ○ trip to the theme park
- ○ gold bracelet
- ○ new sweater

33
- ○ cartoon characters
- ○ underwater ride
- ○ princess's castle

34
- ○ took Robin on a ride
- ○ waved at Robin
- ○ showed Robin a castle

STOP

# UNIT THIRTEEN
## Practice Test 5

Language

**Sample A**

○ ○ ○  STOP

**1**

○ ○ ○

**2**

○ ○ ○

**3**

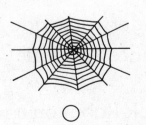 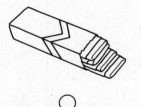 

○ ○ ○

**4**

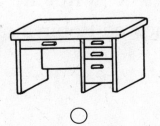  ...

○ ○ ○ STOP

You have 40 minutes to complete this test.

**Sample B**

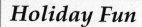 *Holiday Fun*

The Fourth of July

| Watch fireworks | Open presents | Go on a picnic |

○          ○          ○

 STOP

**Sample C**

I like the Fourth of July best.
My family and I like to watch the parade.
After the parade, we go to the park.
To have a picnic.

○ I like the Fourth of July best.

○ After the parade, we go to the park.

○ To have a picnic.

STOP

**Sample D**

We <u>watches</u> the fireworks at night.
The colors light up the sky.

watch              watching         Correct the way it is.
○                    ○                    ○

STOP

## The Pool Party

**5**    ○ when          ○ wish          ○ water

**6**
- ○ the time the party begins
- ○ the size of the pool
- ○ his house number and street name

Dear Sam,

I am having a pool party.
It will be this <u>Friday, August 19.</u>
                        **(1)**
Come to my house at 359 Pine Road.
<u>We will much fun have.</u>
**(2)**

**7**    ○ friday, august 19    ○ friday, August 19    ○ Correct the way it is.

**8**
- ○ We will have much fun.
- ○ We will have fun much.
- ○ Correct the way it is.

▶ GO ON

You <u>need</u> to bring a swimsuit.
     **(1)**
I hope to see you.
Let me know if you <u>arent</u> coming.
                          **(2)**

Your friend,
Matt

**9**    needing        needed        Correct the way it is.
          ○              ○              ○

**10**    aren't        are'nt        Correct the way it is.
          ○              ○              ○

*Pia's Town*

### Table of Contents

**11**    1        2        3
          ○        ○        ○

**12**    10       17       26
          ○        ○        ○

►GO ON◄

In my town, you can visit a cave.
A train takes you under the ground.
A man tells you about the cave.
As you walk on a wide path.

**13**

○ A train takes you under the ground.

○ A man tells you about the cave.

○ As you walk on a wide path.

You can also go to the library.
Each <u>tuesday</u> they have a story time.
     **(1)**
<u>Someone reads</u> a story to the children.
**(2)**
Sometimes they have a puppet play.

**14**     Tues Day        Tuesday        Correct the way it is.
          ○                  ○                  ○

**15**

○ Someone reading

○ Someone read

○ Correct the way it is.

GO ON

*Camp Fun*

**16**
- ○ to tell his friend how to sail
- ○ to tell what he did during the summer
- ○ to tell why he went to camp

Sailing at Camp
I learned to sail a boat at camp.
We ate hot dogs.
First, you have to raise the sails.
The wind fills the sails.

**17**
- ○ I learned to sail a boat at camp.
- ○ We ate hot dogs.
- ○ First, you have to raise the sails.

**18**
- ○ The wind makes the boat move.
- ○ The camp is beside a lake.
- ○ The boat is big.

GO ON

Sometimes the wind does not blow.
Can you guess what happens <u>then</u>
(1)

The boat will not move.
<u>Mr. sanchez</u>, the camp leader, must come get you.
(2)

**19**   then.   then?   then!
○   ○   ○

**20**   Mr. Sanchez   mr. sanchez   Correct the way it is.
○   ○   ○

**Sample E**

    ◯  read

    ◯  two

    ◯  storys

──────────────── 🛑

**21**  ◯  teacher

     ◯  calld

     ◯  name

**22**  ◯  give

     ◯  hir

     ◯  turn

**23**  ◯  carful

     ◯  wake

     ◯  father

**24**  ◯  frend

     ◯  riding

     ◯  bike

**25**  ◯  pick

     ◯  toyes

     ◯  leave

**26**  ◯  fell

     ◯  bumped

     ◯  noze

**27**  ◯  girl

     ◯  three

     ◯  wishs

**28**  ◯  win

     ◯  first

     ◯  prise

**29**  ◯  children

     ◯  playd

     ◯  sun

**30**  ◯  many

     ◯  dayes

     ◯  until

**31**  ◯  packt

     ◯  bags

     ◯  trip

🛑

# Individual Record Form

| | Pages | Number of Questions | Number Right |
|---|---|---|---|
| **Reading Comprehension** | | | |
| Solving Riddles | 23 | 5 | |
| Completing Sentences | 24 | 8 | |
| Reading Stories | 25–28 | 16 | |
| Test | 29–34 | 30 | |
| **Vocabulary and Word Study Skills** | | | |
| Matching Words to Pictures | 35 | 15 | |
| Recognizing Compound Words | 36 | 7 | |
| Choosing Correct Words | 37 | 9 | |
| Recognizing Contractions | 38 | 7 | |
| Matching Word Sounds | 39 | 9 | |
| Recognizing Consonant Sounds | 40 | 8 | |
| Identifying Rhyming Sounds | 41 | 9 | |
| Using Endings to Build New Words | 42 | 10 | |
| Test | 43–49 | 61 | |
| **Math Problem Solving and Procedures** | | | |
| Understanding Numeration | 53 | 6 | |
| Using Whole Numbers, Fractions, and Decimals | 54 | 5 | |
| Working with Patterns and Relationships | 55 | 5 | |
| Working with Statistics and Probability | 56 | 3 | |
| Working with Geometry | 57 | 5 | |
| Working with Measurement | 58 | 5 | |
| Solving Problems | 59 | 3 | |
| Understanding Computation | 60–61 | 9 | |
| Using Computation | 62 | 10 | |
| Test | 63–69 | 39 | |
| **Listening** | | | |
| Listening for Word Meanings | 70 | 12 | |
| Choosing Picture Answers | 71 | 7 | |
| Building Listening Skills | 72 | 9 | |
| Test | 73–75 | 33 | |
| **Language** | | | |
| Listening to Stories | 76 | 4 | |
| Prewriting, Composing, and Editing | 77–82 | 19 | |
| Finding Misspelled Words | 83 | 11 | |
| Test | 84–91 | 29 | |
| **Practice Test 1** | | | |
| Reading Comprehension | 92–99 | 38 | |
| **Practice Test 2** | | | |
| Vocabulary and Word Study Skills | 100–105 | 62 | |
| **Practice Test 3** | | | |
| Part 1: Math Problem Solving | 106–112 | 32 | |
| Part 2: Math Procedures | 113–116 | 26 | |
| **Practice Test 4** | | | |
| Listening | 117–119 | 34 | |
| **Practice Test 5** | | | |
| Language | 120–127 | 31 | |

# Scripts and Answers

- Every skill lesson, Unit Test, and Practice Test begins with sample questions.
- Please do the sample questions together with your child. Check to see that the child has filled in the correct answer space. Go over any questions your child may have.
- As you read the scripts, allow plenty of time for your child to answer the question before moving on to the next item.
- After each exercise, review the questions and answer choices with the child. Discuss why one answer is correct and the others are not correct. Also check to see that the

child has carefully filled in the answer spaces and has completely erased any stray marks.

- In the following scripts, the sections that begin with the word **Say** are to be read out loud to your child. Information in parentheses ( ) is meant for the parent.
- The answers for each page are located immediately following the scripts.
- Make sure your child has his or her cardboard or paper place marker before beginning. It should be a rectangle about 4 inches by 2 inches.

## Unit 2

### Pages 7–10

**Say:** Turn to page 7. In this lesson you will practice answering questions about word meanings. Place your marker under the paragraph that begins with the words "Sometimes you can find out." (Read the paragraph to the child.)

**Say:** Now look at the first passage. Read the passage silently. Then, answer the question that follows: "In this paragraph, the word *wrong* means—*too big … not right … the same*." Read the hint to help you answer the question. You get a clue about the word *wrong* by reading the words *did not fit*. Darken the circle for the correct answer.

**Say:** The correct answer is the second answer choice. *Wrong* means "not right."

**Say:** Now you will practice answering more questions about word meanings. Put your marker under the next row. Beginning on page 7, read each passage carefully and answer the questions that follow. Darken the circle for the correct answer. Answer all the questions on pages 7 through 10. The hints after each question will help you find the right answer. You may now begin.

### Answers: Pages 7–10

**1.** not right, **2.** the best, **3.** looked, **4.** done, **5.** wait, **6.** go around, **7.** not fast, **8.** to say hello

### Pages 11–14

**Say:** Turn to page 11. In this lesson you will practice answering questions about identifying supporting ideas. Place your marker under the sentence that begins with the words "Facts and ideas." (Read the two sentences to the child.)

**Say:** Now look at the first passage. Read the passage silently. Then, answer the question that follows: "Tina and her family went to—*the city … the beach … the country*." Read the hint to help you answer the question. Look at the first sentence. Darken the circle for the correct answer.

**Say:** The correct answer is the second answer choice. Tina and her family went to the beach.

**Say:** Now you will practice answering more questions about identifying supporting ideas. Put your marker under the next row. Beginning on page 11, read each passage carefully and answer the questions that follow. Darken the circle for the right answer. Answer all the questions on pages 11 through 14. The hints after each question will help you find the right answer. You may now begin.

### Answers: Pages 11–12

**1.** the beach, **2.** the man who works at the lighthouse, **3.** 120 feet, **4.** the stump, **5.** different sizes, **6.** It is old.

### Answers: Pages 13–14

**1.** Lucy lost her gloves., **2.** when it was time to go home, **3.** Lucy found her gloves., **4.** Yuko and Rosa were playing outside., **5.** when the girls asked him for help, **6.** The dog was given food.

### Pages 15–16

**Say:** Turn to page 15. In this lesson you will practice answering questions about the main idea of a passage. Now look at the sentence that begins with the words "The main idea." (Read the two sentences to the child.)

**Say:** Place your marker under the first story. Read the passage silently. Then, answer the question that follows: "What is the main idea of this story? *Parrots make great gifts. … It is important to keep your room clean. … Parrots can say things at the wrong time.*" Read the hint to help you answer the question. Think about the whole story. Look at the first paragraph. Darken the circle for the correct answer.

**Say:** The correct answer is the third answer choice. Parrots can say things at the wrong time.

**Say:** Now you will practice answering another question about recognizing the main idea. Place your marker under the next story. On page 16, read the passage carefully and answer the question that follows. The hint after the question will help you find the right answer. Darken the circle for the correct answer. You may now begin.

## Answers: Pages 15–16

1. Parrots can say things at the wrong time., 2. Ricka wants to be an animal doctor.

## Pages 17–20

**Say:** Turn to page 17. In this lesson you will practice answering questions about cause-and-effect relationships and predicting what will happen next. Now look at the sentence that begins with the words "Knowing what happened." (Read the sentence to the child.)

**Say:** Place your marker under the first story. Read the passage silently. Then, answer the question that follows: "Why did Grandma come to visit? *She wanted to move from Japan. … She wanted to see the new baby. … She wanted to take a trip.*" Read the hint to help you answer the question. What happened that made Grandma come to visit? Darken the circle for the correct answer.

**Say:** The correct answer is the second answer choice. Grandma wanted to see the new baby.

**Say:** Now you will practice answering more questions about cause-and-effect relationships and predicting what will happen next. Place your marker under the next row. Beginning on page 17, read each passage carefully and answer the questions that follow. Answer all the questions on pages 17 through 20. The hint after each question will help you find the right answer. Darken the circle for the correct answer. You may now begin.

## Answers: Pages 17–18

1. She wanted to see the new baby., 2. He's a cute little baby., 3. She wants to run faster., 4. She won a race.

## Answers: Pages 19–20

1. Tricia will buy a book or a puzzle., 2. go shopping for a gift

## Pages 21–22

**Say:** Turn to page 21. In this lesson you will practice answering questions about making judgments and reaching conclusions. Place your marker under the sentence that begins with the words "What a character says." (Read the sentence to the child.)

**Say:** Now look at the first passage. Read the passage silently. Then, answer the question that follows: "Why does Patrick want his cat to have a new collar? *The cat will be happier with one. … He is afraid his cat will get lost. … The collar he has now is very old.*" Read the hint to help you answer the question. Why is Patrick worried? Darken the circle for the correct answer.

**Say:** The correct answer is the second answer choice. He is afraid his cat will get lost.

**Say:** Now you will practice answering another question about making judgments and reaching conclusions. Place your marker under the next story. On page 22, read the passage carefully and answer the question that follows. The hint after the question will help you find the right answer. Darken the circle for the correct answer. You may now begin.

## Answers: Pages 21–22

1. He is afraid his cat will get lost., 2. He likes to go to Maine.

# Unit 3

## Page 23

**Say:** Turn to page 23. In this lesson you will practice solving riddles. When you read the two sentences, look at the pictures. Then, darken the circle under the picture that the sentences tell about.

**Say:** Place your marker under the first row. This is Sample A. Look at the two sentences and the pictures of the fly, the bird, and the girl. Listen carefully as I read the sentences: "I cannot fly. I can sing." Darken the circle under the picture that shows what the sentences tell about.

**Say:** The correct answer is the picture of the girl. The girl can sing, but she cannot fly. The bird can sing and fly. The fly cannot sing, but it can fly.

**Say:** Now you will practice solving more riddles. Put your marker under number 1. Do numbers 1 through 5 just as you did Sample A. Darken the circle under the correct answer. You may now begin.

### Answers: Page 23
**Sample A:** picture of the girl, **1.** picture of the Moon, **2.** picture of the shark, **3.** picture of the truck, **4.** picture of the rowboat, **5.** picture of the Sun

## Page 24

**Say:** Turn to page 24. In this lesson you will practice choosing words that best complete sentences about pictures. Look at Sample A with the picture and row of words. Study the picture carefully. Look for clues in the picture to help you choose the correct word. Then, darken the circle under the word that best completes the sentence. Now place your marker under the first row for Sample A. Look at the picture. Listen carefully as I read the first sentence. "Sheila found some—*trees … bees … grass.*" Darken the circle under the word that best completes the sentence.

**Say:** Now look at Sample B and the next row of words. Look at the same picture and listen as I read the second sentence. "She is—*walking … dancing … running.*" Darken the circle under the word that best completes the sentence.

**Say:** In the first sentence, you should have darkened the circle under *bees*. The picture shows that Sheila found some bees. In the second sentence, you should have darkened the circle under *running*. The picture shows Sheila running from the bees.

**Say:** Now you will practice choosing more words that best complete sentences. Do numbers 1 through 8 just as you did Sample A and Sample B. Darken the circle under the correct answer. You may now begin.

### Answers: Page 24
**Sample A:** bees, **Sample B:** running, **1.** lap, **2.** book, **3.** sleep, **4.** soup, **5.** hat, **6.** pet, **7.** bed, **8.** turtle

## Pages 25–28

**Say:** Turn to page 25. In this lesson you will practice answering questions about stories that you read. Carefully read the questions and the answer choices. More than one answer choice may seem correct. Be sure to choose the answer that goes best with the story. Check your answers by looking back in the story.

**Say:** Place your marker under the first row. This is Sample A. Read the story. Then, read the question and the answer choices. "What color is Ben's boat? *red … blue … yellow.*" Darken the circle beside the correct answer.

**Say:** The correct answer is the second choice, *blue*. The third sentence in the story says that Ben's boat is blue. Marta has a red boat, and the person writing the story has a yellow boat.

**Say:** Now you will practice answering more questions about stories that you read. Put your marker under the next row, the one that has the title "Manny Helps Out." Do numbers 1 through 16 just as you did Sample A. Read each story. Then, read the questions and the answer choices that follow. Darken the circle beside the correct answer. If there are no choices, write your answer on the lines. You may now begin.

### Answers: Pages 25–28
**Sample A:** blue, **1.** older than Manny, **2.** He wants to help his dad., **3.** He gets paint on them., **4.** Manny will go out to play., **5.** build things, **6.** a car, **7.** unhappy, **8.** plays with blocks, **9.** It is the end of school., **10.** pizza, **11.** a swimsuit, **12.** call Lila, **13.** two, **14.** love Peppy, **15.** when he wants food, **16.** two children and their new pet

131

## Test: Pages 29–34

**Say:** Turn to the Unit 3 Test on page 29. In this test, you will use the reading skills you have practiced in this unit. This test is divided into three parts. For each part there is a sample exercise. We will work each sample together. In the first part of the test, you will solve riddles.

**Say:** Put your marker under the first row. This is Sample A. Look at the pictures of the seal, the worm, and the dog. Listen carefully as I read the sentences: "I can bark. I cannot run." Darken the circle under the picture that shows what the sentences tell about.

**Say:** The correct answer is the picture of the seal. A seal can bark, but it cannot run.

**Say:** Now you will solve more riddles. Put your marker under number 1. Do numbers 1 through 7 just as you did Sample A. Darken the circle under the correct answer. You may now begin.

**Say:** Now turn to page 30. In this part of the test, you will choose words that best complete sentences that tell something about pictures. Place your marker under the first row of words. This is Sample B. Look at the picture. Listen carefully as I read the sentence: "Ming and Elly are on the—*beach … floor … table*." Darken the circle under the word that best completes the sentence.

**Say:** Now move your marker under the second row of words. This is Sample C. Listen carefully as I read the sentence: "They are—*walking … sleeping … playing*." Darken the circle under the word that best completes the sentence.

**Say:** For Sample B, you should have darkened the circle under the word *beach*, because the picture shows Ming and Elly building a sand castle on the beach. For Sample C, you should have darkened the circle under the word *playing*, because the picture shows them playing on the beach.

**Say:** Now you will choose more words that best complete sentences. Put your marker under the first sentence under the next picture for number 8. Do numbers 8 through 15 just as you did Samples B and C. Darken the circle under the correct answer. You may now begin.

**Say:** Now go to page 31. In the last part of the test, you will answer questions about stories that you read. Put your marker under the first row. This is Sample D. Read the story. Then, read the question and the answer choices that follow. "Who hits the ball? *Marc … Sue Lin … Juan*." Darken the circle beside the correct answer.

**Say:** The correct answer is the second choice, Sue Lin. The second sentence of the story tells you that Sue Lin hit the ball.

**Say:** Now you will practice answering questions about more stories that you read. Put your marker under number 16. Do numbers 16 through 30 just as you did Sample D. Read each story. Then, read the questions and answer choices that follow. Darken the circle next to the correct answer. If there are no choices, write your answer on the lines. You may now begin.

## Answers: Pages 29–34

**Sample A:** seal, **1.** baby, **2.** airplane, **3.** girl, **4.** turtle, **5.** fork, **6.** iron, **7.** shoes, **Sample B:** beach, **Sample C:** playing, **8.** stage, **9.** clap, **10.** over, **11.** tent, **12.** finished, **13.** dress, **14.** fun, **15.** smiling, **Sample D:** Sue Lin, **16.** in the yard, **17.** Its mother was gone., **18.** It was ready to take care of itself., **19.** kind, **20.** a trunk, **21.** 600, **22.** use their trunks, **23.** important, **24.** Springtown Community Center, **25.** 3:30 P.M., **26.** It is free., **27.** a forest, **28.** He fixed its leg and fed it., **29.** The unicorn stayed with the man., **30.** thankful

# Unit 4

## Page 35

**Say:** Turn to page 35. In this lesson you will practice matching words to pictures. Put your marker under the picture and the first row of words. This is Sample A. Look at the picture and read each word. Decide if the word tells about something in the picture. Now listen to the words in Row A: *duck … dog … doll*. Darken the circle under the word that tells about the picture.

**Say:** Now place your marker under the second row of words. This is Sample B. The words in Row B are *stairs … large … ladder*. Study the picture again. Then, darken the circle under the word that tells about the picture.

**Say:** In Sample A, you should have darkened the circle under the word *dog*. *Dog* is the only word that tells about the picture. In Sample B, you should have darkened the circle under the word *ladder*. Only the word *ladder* tells about the picture.

**Say:** Now you will practice finding more words that tell about pictures. Place your marker under the next row for number 1. Do numbers 1 through 15 just as you did Samples A and B. Darken the circle under the correct answer. You may now begin.

## Answers: Page 35
Sample A: dog, **Sample B:** ladder, **1.** boy, **2.** shopping, **3.** foods, **4.** child, **5.** bounce, **6.** ball, **7.** plant, **8.** tree, **9.** shovel, **10.** rake, **11.** leaves, **12.** helping, **13.** door, **14.** steps, **15.** leave

## Page 36
**Say:** Turn to page 36. In this lesson you will practice finding compound words. Put your marker under the first group of words. This is Sample A. A compound word is a word that is made up of two words put together. Look at the words *sometimes*, *counting*, and *hammer*. Darken the circle beside the compound word.

**Say:** The correct answer is the word *sometimes*. *Sometimes* is a compound word made up of the words *some* and *times*. *Counting* and *hammer* are not made up of two words put together.

**Say:** Now you will practice finding more compound words. Put your marker under number 1. Do numbers 1 through 7 just as you did Sample A. Darken the circle beside the correct answer. You may now begin.

## Answers: Page 36
Sample A: sometimes, **1.** peanut, **2.** tugboat, **3.** football, **4.** sundown, **5.** outside, **6.** airplane, **7.** daylight

## Page 37
**Say:** Turn to page 37. In this lesson you will practice matching printed words with words that you hear. Put your marker under Sample A at the top of the first column. Look at the words in Sample A: *rained … raining … rains*. These words are similar, but they do not have the same endings. I will say one of these words and use it in a sentence. You should look at the words, listen to each word, and say the word to yourself. Then, find the word I say. Now listen carefully. Darken the circle beside the word *rained*. It *rained* all morning. *Rained*.

**Say:** The correct answer is the first word, *rained*. Although the word *rain* is a part of each word, *rained* is the word that you heard.

**Say:** Now you will practice matching more printed words with words that you hear. Put your marker under number 1. Do numbers 1 through 9 just as you did Sample A. Listen carefully to the word and the sentence. Then, darken the circle beside the correct answer.

**Say:**

1. Darken the circle beside the word *sang*. Her aunt *sang* beautifully. *Sang*.

2. Place your marker under the next group of words. Darken the circle beside the word *reading*. He is *reading* a book. *Reading*.

3. Place your marker under the next group of words. Darken the circle beside the word *branches*. There was a nest between the *branches*. *Branches*.

4. Place your marker under the next group of words. Darken the circle beside the word *sleepy*. The baby was *sleepy*. *Sleepy*.

5. Move to the top of the next column. Place your marker under the first group of words. Darken the circle beside the word *baked*. Dad *baked* some bread. *Baked*.

6. Place your marker under the next group of words. Darken the circle beside the word *dance*. I watched her *dance* across the stage. *Dance*.

7. Place your marker under the next group of words. Darken the circle beside the word *higher*. Maria jumped *higher* than Rob. *Higher*.

8. Place your marker under the next group of words. Darken the circle beside the word *flash*. We saw a *flash*, then we saw the fire. *Flash*.

9. Place your marker under the last group of words. Darken the circle beside the word *lowest*. The book is on the *lowest* shelf. *Lowest*.

## Answers: Page 37
Sample A: rained, **1.** sang, **2.** reading, **3.** branches, **4.** sleepy, **5.** baked, **6.** dance, **7.** higher, **8.** flash, **9.** lowest

## Page 38
**Say:** Turn to page 38. In this lesson you will practice finding contractions, or shortened forms of two other words. Put your marker under the first group of words. This is Sample A. Look at the words: *I'd … I've … I'm*. Each of these words is a shortened form, or a contraction, of two other words. I will say two words and use them in a sentence. Study the three contractions carefully. Then, silently say the two words that form each contraction. The answer choices may look alike, but only one has the same meaning as the two words that you hear. Listen carefully. Darken the circle beside the word that means *I would*. I *would* like some water. *I would*.

**Say:** The correct answer is the word *I'd*. The contraction *I'd* means "I would." The sentence *I would like some water* has the same meaning as the sentence *I'd like some water*. *I've* means "I have." *I'm* means "I am."

**Say:** Now you will practice finding more contractions. Put your marker under number 1. Do numbers 1 through 7 just as you did Sample A. Listen carefully to the two words and the sentence. Then, darken the circle beside the correct answer.

**Say:**

1. Darken the circle beside the word that means *we are*. *We are* on our way home. *We are*.

2. Place your marker under the next group of words. Darken the circle beside the word that means *she will*. *She will* pick up her toys now. *She will*.

3. Place your marker under the next group of words. Darken the circle beside the word that means *who will*. *Who will* help me? *Who will*.

4. Move to the top of the next column. Place your marker under the first group of words. Darken the circle beside the word that means *we would*. *We would* be pleased for you to join us. *We would*.

5. Place your marker under the next group of words. Darken the circle beside the word that means *has not*. She *has not* called me today. *Has not*.

6. Place your marker under the next group of words. Darken the circle beside the word that means *will not*. The puppy *will not* be quiet. *Will not*.

7. Place your marker under the last group of words. Darken the circle beside the word that means *you will*. *You will* do your best. *You will*.

## Answers: Page 38
**Sample A:** I'd, **1.** we're, **2.** she'll, **3.** who'll, **4.** we'd, **5.** hasn't, **6.** won't, **7.** you'll

## Page 39
**Say:** Turn to page 39. In this lesson you will practice finding words that have the same sounds as words that you hear. Place your marker under the first group of words. This is Sample A. Look at the word *fish* and the three answer choices. Notice that the *sh* in *fish* is underlined. Say the word to yourself. Decide how the underlined part of the word sounds. As you say each answer choice, listen for that sound. Then, darken the circle under the word that has the same sound or sounds as the underlined part of the first word in each row. Now listen carefully. Darken the circle under the word that has the same sound as the underlined *sh* in *fish* … *fish*.

**Say:** The correct answer is the word *dish*. The *sh* in *dish* makes the same sound as the *sh* in *fish*.

**Say:** Now you will practice matching more words that have the same sound or sounds as words you hear. Put your marker under number 1. Do numbers 1 through 9 just as you did Sample A. Listen carefully as I read each word. Then, darken the circle under the correct answer.

**Say:**

1. Darken the circle under the word that has the same sound as the underlined letter in *lift* … *lift*.

2. Place your marker under the next row of words. Darken the circle under the word that has the same sound as the underlined letter in *hid* … *hid*.

3. Place your marker under the next row of words. Darken the circle under the word that has the same sound as the underlined letter in *cat* … *cat*.

4. Place your marker under the next row of words. Darken the circle under the word that has the same sound as the underlined letters in *path* … *path*.

5. Move to the top of the next column. Place your marker under the first row of words. Darken the circle under the word that has the same sound as the underlined letter in *ten* … *ten*.

6. Place your marker under the next row of words. Darken the circle under the word that has the same sound as the underlined letter in *light* … *light*.

7. Place your marker under the next row of words. Darken the circle under the word that has the same sound as the underlined letters in *chase* … *chase*.

8. Place your marker under the next row of words. Darken the circle under the word that has the same sound as the underlined letters in *train* … *train*.

9. Place your marker under the last row of words. Darken the circle under the word that has the same sound as the underlined letter in *face* … *face*.

## Answers: Page 39
**Sample A:** dish, **1.** pin, **2.** mad, **3.** kitten, **4.** third, **5.** today, **6.** bite, **7.** watch, **8.** plane, **9.** state

## Page 40
**Say:** Turn to page 40. In this lesson, you will practice matching names of pictures with words that have the same consonant sounds. Put your marker under the first set of pictures. This is Sample A. Look at the pictures of the star, the number ten, and the Sun. I will say a word. Study the pictures carefully and find the one that begins with the same sound as the word I say. Darken the circle under the choice with the same sound. Now listen carefully. Darken the circle under the picture that begins with the same sounds as *stop* … *stop*.

**Say:** Now place your marker under the first set of words. This is Sample B. Look at the words: *choice* … *witch* … *pitcher*. Darken the circle under the word that ends with the same sound as *pinch* … *pinch*.

**Say:** In Sample A you should have darkened the circle under the picture of the star. *Star* is correct because *star* and *stop* both begin with the *st* sound. In Sample B, you should have darkened the circle under the word *witch*. The word *witch* is correct because *witch* and *pinch* both end with the *ch* sound.

**Say:** Now you will practice matching more consonant sounds. Put your marker on number 1. Do numbers 1 through 8 just as you did Sample A and Sample B. Listen carefully to each statement. Then, darken the circle under the correct answer.

**Say:**

1. First you will listen for beginning sounds. Darken the circle under the picture whose name begins with the same sound as *kind* … *kind*.

2. Place your marker under the next row of pictures. Darken the circle under the picture whose name begins with the same sound as *fill* … *fill*.

3. Place your marker under the next row of words. Darken the circle under the word that begins with the same sound as *hip* … *hip*.

4. Move to the top of the next column. Place your marker under the first row of words. Darken the circle under the word that begins with the same sounds as *there* … *there*.

5. Place your marker under the next row of pictures. Now you will listen for ending sounds. Darken the circle under the picture whose name ends with the same sounds as *part* … *part*.

6. Place your marker under the next row of pictures. Darken the circle under the picture whose name ends with the same sounds as *dump* … *dump*.

7. Place your marker under the next row of words. Darken the circle under the word that ends with the same sounds as *dismiss* … *dismiss*.

8. Place your marker under the last row of words. Now you will listen for words that have the same consonant sound in the middle. Darken the circle under the word that has the same middle sounds as *chilly* … *chilly*.

## Answers: Page 40
**Sample A:** star, **Sample B:** witch, **1.** kitten (cat), **2.** fish, **3.** hatch, **4.** this, **5.** heart, **6.** lamp, **7.** class, **8.** jelly

## Page 41
**Say:** Turn to page 41. In this lesson, you will practice finding words and pictures that rhyme with sounds. Put your marker under the first set of pictures. This is Sample A. There are pictures of the number 1, a chain, and a car. I will say a word. Study the pictures carefully and find the one that rhymes with the word I say. Now listen carefully. Darken the circle under the picture whose name rhymes with *mane* … *mane*.

**Say:** You should have darkened the circle under the picture of the chain. *Chain* rhymes with *mane*.

**Say:** Now you will practice finding more matching words. Put your marker under number 1. Darken the circle under the correct answer as I read each question aloud.

**Say:**

1. Darken the circle under the picture whose name rhymes with *corn* … *corn*.

2. Place your marker under the next row of pictures. Darken the circle under the picture whose name rhymes with *word* … *word*.

3. Place your marker under the next row of words. Darken the circle under the word that rhymes with *loop* … *loop*.

4. Place your marker under the next row of words. Darken the circle under the word that rhymes with *gaze* … *gaze*.

5. Move to the top of the next column. Place your marker under the first row of pictures. Darken the circle under the picture whose name rhymes with *fan* … *fan*.

6. Place your marker under the next row of pictures. Darken the circle under the picture whose name rhymes with *hard* … *hard*.

7. Place your marker under the next row of words. Darken the circle under the word that rhymes with *band* … *band*.

8. Place your marker under the next row of words. Darken the circle under the word that rhymes with *snow* … *snow*.

9. Place your marker under the last row of words. Darken the circle under the word that rhymes with *lamp* … *lamp*.

## Answers: Page 41
**Sample A:** chain, **1.** horn, **2.** bird, **3.** soup, **4.** days, **5.** pan, **6.** card, **7.** hand, **8.** show, **9.** camp

## Page 42

**Say:** Turn to page 42. In this lesson, you will practice adding word endings, or suffixes, to make new words. Put your marker under the first set of words. This is Sample A. Look at the word *fail* and the three choices of word endings. Add each word ending to the end of the word *fail* to try to make a new word. Then, darken the circle underneath the word ending that makes a new word when added to *fail*.

**Say:** You should have darkened the circle under *ing* because *fail* and *ing* make the word *failing*. The endings *ous* and *ness* cannot be added to the word *fail* to make a word.

**Say:** Now you will practice making other new words by adding endings. Put your marker on number 1. Darken the circle under the correct answer as I read each question aloud.

**Say:**

1. Look at the word *cheer* in row 1. Darken the circle under the ending that can be added to make a new word.

2. Place your marker under the word *perfect* in row 2. Darken the circle under the ending that can be added to make a new word.

3. Place your marker under the word *smooth* in row 3. Darken the circle under the ending that can be added to make a new word.

4. Place your marker under the word *sad* in row 4. Darken the circle under the ending that can be added to make a new word.

5. Place your marker under the word *final* in row 5. Darken the circle under the ending that can be added to make a new word.

6. Move to the top of the next column. Place your marker under the word *perform* in row 6. Darken the circle under the ending that can be added to make a new word.

7. Place your marker under the word *enjoy* in row 7. Darken the circle under the ending that can be added to make a new word.

8. Place your marker under the word *great* in row 8. Darken the circle under the ending that can be added to make a new word.

9. Place your marker under the word *fool* in row 9. Darken the circle under the ending that can be added to make a new word.

10. Place your marker under the word *joy* in row 10. Darken the circle under the ending that can be added to make a new word.

## Answers: Page 42
**Sample A:** ing, **1.** ful, **2.** ly, **3.** er, **4.** ness, **5.** ly, **6.** er, **7.** able, **8.** ness, **9.** ish, **10.** ful

## Test: Pages 43–49

**Say:** Turn to the Unit 4 Test on page 43. In this test you will use the vocabulary and word reading skills we have practiced in this unit. Put your marker under the picture and the words in Sample A. Study the picture. Look at the words: *doctor … dragon … horse*. Darken the circle under the word that tells about the picture.

**Say:** You should have darkened the circle under the word *dragon* because the picture shows a child dressed like a dragon.

**Say:** Now put your marker under the next row of words. Look at the words in Sample B. The words are *fire … water … smoke*. Darken the circle under the word that tells about the picture.

**Say:** You should have darkened the circle under the word *smoke* because the picture shows smoke coming from the dragon's nostril.

**Say:** Now put your marker under the next row of words. Look at the words in Sample C. The words are *costume … crowd … coat*. Darken the circle under the word that tells about the picture.

**Say:** You should have darkened the circle under the word *costume* because the picture shows a child wearing a dragon costume.

**Say:** Now you will find more words that tell about pictures. Place your marker under the next picture and the row of words for number 1. Do numbers 1 through 15 just as you did the samples. Darken the circle under the correct answer. You may now begin.

**Say:** Now turn to page 44. In this part of the test, you will find compound words. Put your marker under Sample D. Look at the words *fiddle*, *rather*, and *bedroom*. Darken the circle beside the compound word.

**Say:** You should have darkened the circle beside *bedroom* because *bedroom* is a compound word made up of the words *bed* and *room*.

**Say:** Now you will find more compound words. Put your marker under number 16. Do numbers 16 through 19 just as you did Sample D. Darken the circle beside the compound word. You may now begin.

**Say:** Now go to the top of the second column. In this part of the test, you will match printed words with words you hear. Put your marker under Sample E. Look at the words *coldest … colder … cold*. Darken the circle beside the word *coldest*. Yesterday was the *coldest* day of the year. *Coldest*.

**Say:** You should have darkened the circle beside *coldest*. Although *cold* is a part of each word, *coldest* is the correct answer.

**Say:** Now you will match more printed words with words that you hear. Put your marker under number 20. Do numbers 20 through 23 just as you did Sample E. Listen carefully to the word and the sentence. Then, darken the circle beside the correct answer.

**Say:**

20. Darken the circle beside the word *clearly*. She wrote her name *clearly*. *Clearly*.

21. Place your marker under the next group of words. Darken the circle beside the word *careful*. Please be *careful* when you cross the street. *Careful*.

22. Place your marker under the next group of words. Darken the circle beside the word *quickly*. We got dressed *quickly*. *Quickly*.

23. Place your marker under the last group of words. Darken the circle beside the word *friendly*. We moved to a *friendly* neighborhood. *Friendly*.

**Say:** Now turn to page 45. In this part of the test, you will find contractions. Put your marker under Sample F. Look at the contractions *hadn't … haven't … hasn't*. I will say two words and use them in a sentence. You will find the contraction that has the same meaning as the two words I say. Listen carefully. Darken the circle beside the word that means *have not*. We *have not* been to the museum. *Have not*.

**Say:** You should have darkened the circle beside *haven't* because *haven't* is the contraction of the words *have not*.

**Say:** Now you will find more contractions. Put your marker under number 24. Do numbers 24 through 27 just as you did Sample F. Listen carefully. Then, darken the circle beside the correct answer.

**Say:**

24. Darken the circle beside the word that means *is not*. The pie *is not* baked yet. *Is not*.

25. Place your marker under the next group of words. Darken the circle beside the word that means *that is*. *That is* the truth. *That is*.

26. Place your marker under the next group of words. Darken the circle beside the word that means *he would*. *He would* like to join us. *He would*.

27. Place your marker under the last group of words. Darken the circle beside the word that means *they are*. *They are* late. *They are*.

**Say:** Now find Sample G at the top of the second column. In this part of the test, you will match words that have the same sound or sounds as words that you hear. Put your marker under Sample G. Look at the word *broom*. Notice that the letters *b* and *r* in *broom* are underlined. Listen carefully. Darken the circle under the word that has the same sound as the underlined letters in *broom*.

**Say:** You should have darkened the circle under *brand*. *Brand* has the same sound as the underlined letters in *broom*.

**Say:** Now you will match more words that have the same sound or sounds as words that you hear. Put your marker under number 28. Do numbers 28 through 31 just as you did Sample G. Listen carefully. Then, darken the circle under the correct answer.

**Say:**

28. Darken the circle under the word that has the same sound as the underlined letters in *good … good*.

29. Place your marker under the next group of words. Darken the circle under the word that has the same sounds as the underlined letters in *shower … shower*.

30. Place your marker under the next group of words. Darken the circle under the word that has the same sound as the underlined letters in *tear … tear*.

31. Place your marker under the last group of words. Darken the circle under the word that has the same sounds as the underlined letters in *cream … cream*.

**Say:** Turn to page 46. In this part of the test, you will practice finding consonant sounds. Look at Sample H. There are pictures of a rocket, a drum, and a dinosaur. Darken the circle under the picture whose name begins with the same sounds as *drill … drill*.

**Say:** The circle under the picture of the drum should be darkened because *drum* and *drill* begin with the same sounds.

**Say:** Now you will practice matching more sounds. Put your marker on number 32. Do numbers 32 through 46 the way you did Sample H. Darken the circle under the correct answer as I read each question aloud.

**Say:**

32. Darken the circle under the picture whose name begins with the same sound as *giant … giant*.

33. Place your marker under the next group of pictures. Darken the circle under the picture whose name begins with the same sound as *grow … grow*.

34. Place your marker under the next group of words. Darken the circle under the word that begins with the same sound as *free … free*.

35. Move to the top of the next column. Place your marker under the first group of words. Darken the circle under the word that begins with the same sounds as *twelve … twelve.*

36. Place your marker under the next group of words. Darken the circle under the word that begins with the same sounds as *swim … swim.*

37. Place your marker under the next group of words. Darken the circle under the word that begins with the same sounds as *blanket … blanket.*

38. Place your marker under the last group of words. Darken the circle under the word that begins with the same sounds as *key … key.*

Say: Turn to page 47. Now you will match sounds at the ends of words. Put your marker on number 39. Darken the circle under each correct answer as I read each question aloud.

Say:

39. Darken the circle under the picture whose name ends with the same sounds as *learn … learn.*

40. Place your marker under the next group of pictures. Darken the circle under the picture whose name ends with the same sound as *mean … mean.*

41. Place your marker under the next group of pictures. Darken the circle under the picture whose name ends with the same sound as *racket … racket.*

42. Place your marker under the next group of words. Darken the circle under the word whose name ends with the same sounds as *rough … rough.*

43. Place your marker at the top of the next column. Darken the circle under the word whose name ends with the same sounds as *build … build.*

Say: Now you will practice matching sounds in the middle of words. Listen carefully. Put your marker on number 44.

Say:

44. Darken the circle under the word that has the same sounds in the middle as *dagger … dagger.*

45. Place your marker under the next group of words. Darken the circle under the word that has the same sounds in the middle as *muddy … muddy.*

46. Place your marker under the last group of words. Darken the circle under the word that has the same sounds in the middle as *sooner … sooner.*

Say: Now turn to page 48. In this part of the test, you will practice finding rhyming words. Place your marker on Sample I. Darken the circle under the picture that rhymes with *hot … hot.*

Say: The circle under the picture of the pot should be darkened because *pot* rhymes with *hot.* Now you will find more rhyming words. Place your marker on number 47. Do numbers 47 through 54 as you did Sample I. Darken the circle under the correct answer as I read each question aloud.

Say:

47. Darken the circle under the picture that rhymes with *near … near.*

48. Place your marker on the next group of pictures. Darken the circle under the picture that rhymes with *meal … meal.*

49. Place your marker on the next group of words. Darken the circle under the word that rhymes with *hair … hair.*

50. Place your marker at the top of the next column. Darken the circle under the word that rhymes with *maze … maze.*

51. Place your marker on the next group of words. Darken the circle under the word that rhymes with *wood … wood.*

52. Place your marker on the next group of words. Darken the circle under the word that rhymes with *bread … bread.*

53. Place your marker on the next group of words. Darken the circle under the word that rhymes with *glue … glue.*

54. Place your marker on the last group of words. Darken the circle under the word that rhymes with *slam … slam.*

Say: Now turn to page 49. In this part of the test, you will practice putting two words together to form a new word. Put your marker on Sample J. Darken the circle under the ending that can be added to the word *fear* to make a new word.

Say: The circle under the ending *less* should be darkened because the ending *less* can be added to the word *fear* to make the new word *fearless.* Now you will make more new words. Put your marker on number 55. Do numbers 55 through 61 as you did in Sample J. Darken the circle under the correct answer as I read each question aloud.

Say:

55. Look at the word *hope* in row 55. Darken the circle under the ending that can be added to make a new word.

56. Look at the word *dark* in row 56. Darken the circle under the ending that can be added to make a new word.

**57.** Look at the word *follow* in row 57. Darken the circle under the ending that can be added to make a new word.

**58.** Look at the word *scold* in row 58. Darken the circle under the ending that can be added to make a new word.

**59.** Look at the word *rough* in row 59. Darken the circle under the ending that can be added to make a new word.

**60.** Look at the word *laugh* in row 60. Darken the circle under the ending that can be added to make a new word.

**61.** Look at the word *sing* in row 61. Darken the circle under the ending that can be added to make a new word.

**Answers: Pages 43–49**
**Sample A:** dragon, **Sample B:** smoke,
**Sample C:** costume, **1.** pull, **2.** wagon, **3.** puppy,
**4.** wash, **5.** soap, **6.** dishes, **7.** rain, **8.** clouds,
**9.** storm, **10.** lady, **11.** bowl, **12.** stir, **13.** picnic,
**14.** eating, **15.** friends, **Sample D:** bedroom,
**16.** teacup, **17.** raincoat, **18.** anyone, **19.** seashell,
**Sample E:** coldest, **20.** clearly, **21.** careful,
**22.** quickly, **23.** friendly, **Sample F:** haven't, **24.** isn't,
**25.** that's, **26.** he'd, **27.** they're, **Sample G:** brand,
**28.** book, **29.** loud, **30.** wear, **31.** week,
**Sample H:** drum, **32.** giraffe, **33.** grapes, **34.** front,
**35.** twig, **36.** sweep, **37.** blossom, **38.** kiss, **39.** corn,
**40.** seven, **41.** basket, **42.** chief, **43.** fold, **44.** wagon,
**45.** sadden, **46.** finish, **Sample I:** pot, **47.** deer,
**48.** wheel, **49.** bear, **50.** ways, **51.** good, **52.** head,
**53.** shoe, **54.** clam, **Sample J:** less, **55.** ful, **56.** er,
**57.** ing, **58.** ing, **59.** est, **60.** ed, **61.** er

# Unit 5

**Answers: Page 51**
**Step 1:** Will Tania's fish fit in the new tank?,
**Step 2:** The tank holds 15 fish. There are 6 goldfish and 5 guppies., **Step 3:** Add to see how many fish Tania has., **Step 4:** 6 + 5 = 11. There are 11 fish, and the tank can hold 15 fish. The tank is large enough., **Step 5:** Yes.

**Answers: Page 52**
**Step 1:** At what time will he begin to feed the 3rd lion?,
**Step 2:** It takes 5 minutes to feed each lion. Kyle starts feeding the lions at 12:00 noon., **Step 3:** draw a picture or use a clock, **Step 4:** 1st lion fed at 12:00, 2nd lion fed at 12:05, 3rd lion fed at 12:10, **Step 5:** Yes.

# Unit 6

**Page 53**
(Distribute scratch paper to the child to use to work the problems.)

**Say:** Turn to page 53. In this lesson you will practice choosing pictures and numbers that answer math problems. Listen carefully. When I read a problem, look at each picture or number for the problem.

Think carefully about the information in the problem. Then, find the picture or numbers that answer the problem you hear. Place your marker under the first row, the one with the picture of the paper clips. This is Sample A. Now listen carefully. Darken the circle under the number that tells how many paper clips are shown.

**Say:** You should have darkened the circle under the first number. There are 2 tens and 4 ones, or 24 paper clips shown in the picture. The correct answer is 24.

**Say:** Now you will practice choosing more pictures and numbers that answer math problems about numbers and objects. Do numbers 1 through 6 just as you did Sample A. Listen carefully to each problem. Then, choose your answer from the pictures or numbers given for the problem. If no choices are given, write your answer on the lines. Now we will begin. Place your marker under the first row below the Sample A and the stop sign. This is number 1. Look at the numbers in the row.

**Say:**

1. Darken the circle under the number ninety-four.

2. Place your marker under the next row. Darken the circle under the number that has the 2 in the tens place.

3. Place your marker under the next row. Darken the circle under the bird that is third from the clouds.

4. Place your marker under the next row, the one with the blocks. There are three stacks of blocks and some extra blocks. Darken the circle under the number that tells how many blocks there are altogether.

5. Place your marker under the next row. Write the number that is ten less than the number on the door.

6. Place your marker under the last row on the page. Look at the boxes with the dots. Darken the circle under the box with the least number of dots.

## Answers: Page 53
**Sample A:** 24, **1.** 94, **2.** 427, **3.** The second circle should be darkened., **4.** 32, **5.** 11, **6.** The third circle should be darkened.

## Page 54
(Distribute scratch paper to the child to use to work the problems.)

**Say:** Turn to page 54. In this lesson, you will practice choosing pictures and numbers that answer math questions about numbers and fractions. Place your marker under the first row, the one with the rectangles. This is Sample A. Now listen carefully. Find the rectangle that is divided into three equal parts. Darken the circle under the rectangle that is divided into three equal parts.

**Say:** You should have darkened the circle under the second rectangle. The second rectangle is the only one that is divided into three equal parts. The other rectangles are divided into more than three equal parts.

**Say:** Now you will practice choosing more pictures and numbers that answer math questions about numbers and fractions. Do numbers 1 through 5 just as you did Sample A. Listen carefully to each problem. Then, choose your answer from the pictures or numbers given for the problem. Now we will begin. Place your marker under the row for number 1. Look at the pots of flowers.

**Say:**

1. Darken the circle under the pot that has three fifths of the flowers shaded.

2. Place your marker under the next row. Darken the circle under the shape that is divided into four equal parts.

3. Place your marker under the next row. Be sure to move your marker so you can see all the answer choices. Darken the circle under the numbers that mean the same as eight plus two.

4. Place your marker under the next row. Look at the number sentence. Darken the circle under the number sentence that is in the same fact family as the number sentence in the box.

5. Place your marker under the last row on the page. Darken the circle under the number that goes in the box to make the number sentence correct.

## Answers: Page 54
**Sample A:** The circle under the second rectangle should be darkened., **1.** The first circle should be darkened., **2.** The fourth circle should be darkened., **3.** $2 + 8$, **4.** $7 - 3 = 4$, **5.** 5

## Page 55
(Distribute scratch paper to the child to use to work the problems.)

**Say:** Turn to page 55. In this lesson you will practice choosing pictures and numbers that answer math questions about numbers and patterns. Place your marker under the first row, the one with the numbers in the boxes. This is Sample A. Now listen carefully. These numbers count by fives. Darken the circle under the number that belongs in the empty box.

**Say:** You should have darkened the circle under the second number, 85. When you count by fives, you count 75, 80, 85, and 90.

**Say:** Now you will practice choosing more pictures and numbers that answer math questions about numbers and patterns. Do numbers 1 through 5 just as you did Sample A. Listen carefully to each problem. Then, choose your answer from the pictures or numbers given for the problem. Now we will begin. Place your marker under the row for number 1, the one with the numbers in the boxes. Be sure to move your marker so you can see all the answer choices.

**Say:**

1. Look at the numbers in the boxes. Darken the circle under the number that belongs in the empty box.

2. Place your marker under the next row. Mrs. Inez numbered all the playground balls. Darken the circle under the ball that Mrs. Inez will number twenty-nine.

3. Place your marker under the next row, the one with the books. Listen carefully. Jason had read eighteen books. He will earn a prize for reading twenty books. He got some more books from the library. Darken the circle under the book that is number twenty.

4. Place your marker under the next row. Darken the circle under the two shapes that come next in this pattern.

5. Place your marker under the last row on the page. Suki chooses cards to make a number pattern. Darken the circle under the card Suki will choose next.

## Answers: Page 55
**Sample A:** 85, **1.** 12, **2.** The second circle should be darkened., **3.** The second circle should be darkened., **4.** The third circle should be darkened., **5.** The third circle should be darkened.

## Page 56
(Distribute scratch paper to the child to use to work the problems.)

**Say:** Turn to page 56. In this lesson you will practice choosing pictures and numbers that answer math questions about graphs, charts, and simple probability. Place your marker under the graph. This is Sample A. Look at the graph. Now listen carefully. Which student has collected the most stars for being a helper? Darken the circle under the name of the student who has collected the most stars.

**Say:** You should have darkened the circle under the last name, Dante. If you count the stars in each row, you find Ariana has four stars, Beata has one star, and Charles has three stars. Dante has the most stars.

**Say:** Now you will practice choosing more pictures and numbers that answer math questions about charts, graphs, and pictures. Do numbers 1 through 3 just as you did Sample A. Listen carefully to each problem. Then, choose your answer from the pictures or numbers given for the problem, or write your answer on the lines. Now we will begin. Place your marker under the row for number 1.

**Say:**

1. Listen carefully. Karen, Ling, Delia, and Steven played games. They used tally marks to show how many games they won. Darken the circle under the name of the person who won five games.

2. Place your marker under the next row. Look carefully at the table. Jerry and Toby kept count of the kinds and numbers of books they read. Write the number that tells how many animal stories Toby read.

3. Place your marker under the last row on the page. Ron played a game with tile shapes. He put one square, four triangles, six circles, and two diamonds into a box. Without looking into the box, which shape will Ron most likely pick? He put into a box one square, four triangles, six circles, and two diamonds. Darken the circle under the shape Ron will most likely pick from the box.

## Answers: Page 56
**Sample A:** Dante, **1.** Ling, **2.** 5, **3.** The third circle should be darkened.

## Page 57
(Distribute scratch paper to the child to use to work the problems.)

**Say:** Turn to page 57. In this lesson you will practice choosing pictures that answer math questions about shapes. Place your marker under the first row. This is Sample A. Now listen carefully. Darken the circle under the picture that can be folded on the dotted line so that the parts on each side of the line match perfectly.

**Say:** You should have darkened the circle for the butterfly. The parts on each side of the dotted line of the butterfly are exactly the same. The parts on each side of the dotted line of the car, the wagon, and the turtle are not the same.

**Say:** Now you will practice choosing more pictures that answer math questions about shapes. Do numbers 1 through 5 just as you did Sample A. Listen carefully to each problem. Then, choose your answer from the pictures given for the problem. Now we will begin. Place your marker under the row for number 1.

**Say:**

1. Look at the shape at the beginning of the row. Darken the circle under the shape that is exactly the same as the shape at the beginning of the row.

2. Place your marker under the next row. Darken the circle under the shape that is a square divided into four triangles.

3. Place your marker under the next row. Darken the circle under the shape that has three sides.

4. Place your marker under the next row. Look at the picture of the shape at the beginning of the row. Darken the circle under the shape that is the same as the first shape but is larger than the first shape in the row.

5. Place your marker under the last row on the page. Look at the shape at the beginning of the row. Darken the circle under the shape that is the same shape but is larger.

## Answers: Page 57
**Sample A:** butterfly, **1.** The first circle should be darkened., **2.** The fourth circle should be darkened., **3.** The third circle should be darkened., **4.** The third circle should be darkened., **5.** The second circle should be darkened.

## Page 58
(Distribute scratch paper to the child to use to work the problems.)

**Say:** Turn to page 58. In this lesson you will practice choosing pictures, words, and numbers that answer math questions about measurement. Place your marker under the first row, the one with the crayon. This is Sample A. Now listen carefully. Use your inch ruler to measure the length of the crayon. Darken the circle under the number that tells the length of the crayon.

**Say:** You should have darkened the second circle, 4 inches. The crayon is 4 inches long.

**Say:** Now you will practice choosing more pictures, words, and numbers that answer math questions about measurement. Do numbers 1 through 5 just as you did Sample A. Listen carefully to each problem. Then, choose your answer from the pictures or numbers given for the problem, or write your answer on the lines. Now we will begin. Place your marker under the row for number 1, the one with the coins. Be sure to move your marker so you can see all of the answer choices.

**Say:**

1. Alfredo found ten cents. Darken the circle under the coin that shows ten cents.

2. Place your marker under the row for number 2. Cathy measures her pencil using paper clips. Darken the circle under the number that tells about how many paper clips long the pencil is.

3. Place your marker under the next row. Darken the circle under the unit that is the best to use to measure the weight of a pencil.

4. Place your marker under the next row, the one with the clock. Uri looks at the clock. He goes to bed at this time each night. Darken the circle under the number that tells the time that Uri goes to bed.

5. Place your marker under the last row on the page. Look at the picture of the calendar. Mr. Tran's garden club meets on the third Saturday of each month. Write the number that is the third Saturday of November.

## Answers: Page 58
**Sample A:** 4 inches, **1.** picture of the dime, **2.** 5, **3.** ounces, **4.** 9:30, **5.** 18

## Page 59
(Distribute scratch paper to the child to use to work the problems.)

**Say:** Turn to page 59. In this lesson you will practice choosing numbers and number sentences that answer math questions you hear. Place your marker under the first row, the one with the pictures of the bananas and apples. This is Sample A. Now listen carefully. Darla went food shopping. First, she put eight bananas in the basket. Then, she put five apples in the basket. How many bananas and apples did Darla put into the basket altogether? Darken the circle beside the number sentence that shows how to find the number of bananas and apples that Darla put into her basket.

**Say:** You should have darkened the circle beside the number sentence, $8 + 5 = \square$. The sentence reads, *eight plus five equals blank*. The word *altogether* tells you to add. Darla had eight bananas and five apples. To find how many Darla had altogether, you would use the number sentence $8 + 5 = \square$.

**Say:** Now you will practice choosing more number sentences and numbers that answer math questions you hear. Do numbers 1 through 3 just as you did Sample A. Listen carefully to each problem. Then, choose your answer from the number sentences or numbers given for the problem. Now we will begin. Place your marker under the row for number 1. Be sure to move your marker so you can see all the answer choices.

**Say:**

1. Look at the numbers. Listen to this riddle about a number. I am thinking of a number that is more than twelve and less than twenty-five. It has a three in it. What number am I thinking of? It is more than twelve and less than twenty-five. It has a three in it. Darken the circle under the number that I am thinking of.

**2.** Place your marker under the next row. Listen to this riddle about a number. I am thinking of a number that is less than thirty-eight. You say its name when you count by fives. It has a two in it. What number am I thinking of? It is less than thirty-eight, you say its name when you count by fives, and it has a two in it. Darken the circle under the number that I am thinking of.

**3.** Place your marker under the last row on the page. Look at the picture of the ducks. Theodore saw nine ducks in the pond in the park. Then, four of the ducks swam away to the other side of the pond. How many ducks were left? Darken the circle beside the number sentence that shows how to find the number of ducks that were left.

**Answers: Page 59**
**Sample A:** 8 + 5 = □, **1.** 23, **2.** 20, **3.** 9 − 4 = □

## Pages 60–61
(Distribute scratch paper to the child to use to work the problems.)

**Say:** Turn to page 60. In this lesson you will practice adding and subtracting numbers to answer word problems you hear. Place your marker under the first row, the one with the picture of the turtles. This is Sample A. Look at the numbers in the row. These are the answer choices. In some problems, you will find that the answer is not among the choices given. If the answer is not given, then darken the circle under *NH* for *not here*. Now listen carefully. Selena had four turtles. She got two more for her birthday. How many turtles did she have altogether? Darken the circle under the number that tells how many turtles Selena has altogether. If the answer is not given, then darken the circle under *NH* for *not here*.

**Say:** You should have darkened the circle under the number 6. Four turtles plus two turtles equal six turtles altogether. The correct answer is 6.

**Say:** Now you will practice adding and subtracting more numbers that answer word problems you hear. Do problems 1 through 9 just as you did Sample A. Listen very carefully to each problem. I will say each problem only once. Find the correct answer given among the answer choices. The last answer in each problem is *NH* for *not here*. This means the answer does not appear as one of the answer choices. If you add or subtract the problems and find that the answer is not among the answer choices, darken the circle for *NH*. If there are no choices, write your answer on the lines. Now we will begin. Place your marker under the first row for number 1.

**Say:**

**1.** Ted saw ten ducks swimming in the pond. He saw five ducks beside the pond. How many ducks did Ted see altogether? Darken the circle under the number that tells how many ducks Ted saw altogether.

**2.** Place your marker under the next row for number 2. Ira put seven oranges in a bag. He put twelve oranges into another bag. How many oranges did Ira put into the bags altogether? Darken the circle under the number that tells how many oranges Ira put into bags.

**3.** Place your marker under the next row for number 3. Mrs. Ling has fifteen calculators on a shelf in her store. She put thirteen more calculators on the shelf. How many calculators are on the shelf in all? Darken the circle under the number that tells how many calculators are on the shelf in all.

**4.** Place your marker under the last row on the page. Listen carefully to this story. Tamiko has five plain shirts. She has three striped shirts. How many shirts does she have altogether? Write the number that tells how many shirts Tamiko has altogether.

**Say:** Now go to page 61. Now we will continue the lesson. Place your marker under the first row for number 5.

**Say:**

**5.** Nathan was collecting lightning bugs. He put five of them into a matchbox but forgot to close the lid. Three lightning bugs flew away. How many lightning bugs does Nathan have left? Write the number that tells how many lightning bugs are left.

**6.** Place your marker under the next row for number 6. José has twenty-nine miniature toy cars. He has six miniature toy trucks. How many more cars than trucks does José have? Darken the circle under the number that tells how many more cars than trucks José has.

**7.** Place your marker under the next row for number 7. Laverne can fit sixteen stamps on a page in her stamp album. She has a page with only eight stamps. How many more stamps can Laverne fit on the page? Darken the circle under the number that tells how many more stamps can fit on the page.

**8.** Place your marker under the row for number 8. Coach Nelson ordered forty-five baseball caps. She gave out eleven caps the first day. How many baseball caps does she have left? Darken the circle under the number that tells how many caps she has left.

9. Place your marker under the last row on the page. A book shop sold fifty-eight books in the morning and forty-two books in the afternoon. How many more books did the book shop sell in the morning than the afternoon? Darken the circle under the number that tells how many more books the store sold in the morning than in the afternoon.

## Answers: Pages 60–61
**Sample A:** 6, **1.** 15, **2.** 19, **3.** NH, **4.** 8, **5.** 2, **6.** 23, **7.** 8, **8.** 34, **9.** 16

## Page 62
(Distribute scratch paper to the child to use to work the problems.)

**Say:** Turn to page 62. In this lesson you will practice adding and subtracting numbers. When you read a problem, look at the sign to see if you should add or subtract. Then, work the problem. You may use the scratch paper to work the problem or you may do the problem in your head. Then, find the number that answers the problem. Place your marker under the first row. This is Sample A. Look at the answer choices given in Sample A. In some problems you will find that the answer is not among the choices given. If the answer is not given, then darken the circle under *NH* for *not here*. If there are no choices, write your answer on the lines. Now listen carefully. You are asked to add two and five. Work the problem on the scratch paper. Then, darken the circle for the correct answer.

**Say:** You should have darkened the circle under *NH*. When you add two and five, the answer is seven. Since 7 is not given as one of the answer choices, the correct answer is *NH*.

**Say:** Now you will practice adding and subtracting more numbers. Do problems 1 through 10 on your own. Read each problem carefully. Work the problem on the scratch paper. Then, darken the circle for the correct answer. If the correct answer is not given, darken the circle for *NH*, *not here*. If there are no choices, write your answer on the lines. You may now begin.

## Answers: Page 62
**Sample A:** NH, **1.** 14, **2.** 10, **3.** 15, **4.** 68, **5.** 57, **6.** 3, **7.** 9, **8.** 40, **9.** 57, **10.** 430

## Test: Pages 63–69
(Distribute scratch paper to the child to use to work the problems. Also distribute inch and centimeter rulers to the child.)

**Say:** Turn to the Unit 6 Test on page 63. In this test you will use your math skills to choose pictures and numbers that answer math questions. Place your marker under the first row, the one with the rake. This is Sample A. Now listen carefully. Darken the circle for the number that tells about how many leaves long the rake is.

**Say:** You should have darkened the circle under the third number, 9. If you look at the four leaves along the top of the rake, you can guess that the total length of the rake is about 9 leaves long.

**Say:** Now place your marker under the next row, the one with the picture of apples. Be sure to move your marker so you can see all of the answer choices. This is Sample B. Listen carefully. Darken the circle under the number that tells exactly how many apples are shown in the picture.

**Say:** You should have darkened the circle under the first number, 28. There are 28 apples in the picture.

**Say:** Now you will choose more pictures and numbers that answer math questions. Do numbers 1 through 21 just as you did the samples. Listen carefully to each problem. Then, choose your answer from the pictures or numbers given in the row. If there are no numbers or pictures, write your answer on the lines. Place your marker under the row for number 1.

**Say:**
1. Write the number that goes in the box to make the number sentence correct.

2. Place your marker under the row for number 2. Darken the circle under the two numbers that both have a three in the ones place.

3. Place your marker under the next row. Darken the circle under the number which is more than forty-nine and less than seventy-two.

4. Place your marker under the last row on the page. Darken the circle under the number that means the same as 20 + 5.

**Say:** Now turn to page 64. Now we will continue the test. Place your marker under the first row, number 5.

**Say:**
5. Look at the number sentence in the box. Darken the circle under the number sentence that is in the same fact family as the number sentence in the box.

6. Place your marker under the row for number 6. Darken the circle under the circle that has one sixth shaded.

7. Place your marker under the next row, the one with the cakes. Darken the circle under the cake that shows two thirds of the candles lit.

8. Place your marker under the next row. Darken the circle under the triangle that has been divided into halves.

9. Place your marker under the next row. Write the number that belongs in the empty box when counting by fives.

10. Place your marker under the next row. Listen carefully. Mr. Carlos delivers mail. He has a letter that needs to be delivered to mailbox sixty-eight. Darken the circle under the mailbox to which Mr. Carlos will deliver the letter.

11. Place your marker under the last row on the page. Look at the children in line. There are sixty-two children inside the circus tent. Darken the circle under the child who will be counted as sixty-four.

**Say:** Now turn to page 65. Now we will continue the test. Place your marker under the first row, number 12. Be sure to move your marker so you can see all of the answer choices.

**Say:**

12. Darken the circle under the shape that is exactly the same as the one at the beginning of the row.

13. Place your marker under the next row, the one with the graph with the kittens. The pet store made a graph to show the number of kittens sold each day during one week. Write the number that tells how many kittens were sold on Thursday.

14. Place your marker under the row for number 14. Darken the circle under the triangle that is divided into two triangles.

15. Place your marker under the next row. Lana is making a cover for a booklet. There are several colors of paper from which to choose. There are nine red sheets, three blue sheets, two orange sheets, and four yellow sheets. If Lana does not look at the paper when she chooses, which color will she most likely get? There are nine red, three blue, two orange, and four yellow sheets. Darken the circle under the color that Lana will most likely choose.

16. Place your marker under the last row on the page. Darken the circle under the shape that comes next in the pattern.

**Say:** Now turn to page 66. Now we will continue the test. Place your marker under the first row, number 17.

**Say:**

17. Listen to this riddle about a number. I am thinking of a number that is more than eight and less than twenty. It has a nine in it. What number am I thinking of? It is more than eight and less than twenty, and has a nine in it. Darken the circle under the number that I am thinking of.

18. Place your marker under the next row, the one with the pictures of the groups of coins. Be sure to move your marker so you can see all of the answer choices. Beth needs twenty-five cents to buy milk. Darken the circle beside the group of coins that shows twenty-five cents.

19. Place your marker under the next row, the one with the picture of the frogs. Look at the picture of the frogs. Listen to this story. Four frogs are sitting on a log. Two more frogs jump onto the log. How many frogs are now on the log? Four frogs are sitting on a log, and two more frogs jump on the log. Darken the circle beside the number sentence that shows how to find the number of frogs that are now on the log.

20. Place your marker under the row for number 20. Use your centimeter ruler to measure the paintbrush. Write the number that tells the length of the paintbrush in centimeters.

21. Place your marker under the last row on the page. Darken the circle under the shape that has exactly four corners.

**Say:** Now turn to page 67. Now we will continue the test. In this part of the test you will add or subtract numbers in math problems you hear or read. The section is divided into two parts. There is a sample for each part. We will work the samples together. Place your marker under the first row, the one with the pictures of the envelopes. This is Sample C. Now listen carefully. Gloria is having a birthday party. She is sending invitations to nine friends. Gloria has addressed seven invitations. How many more invitations does Gloria need to address? She is inviting nine friends and has addressed seven invitations. Darken the circle under the number that tells how many more invitations Gloria needs to address. If the correct answer is not given, darken the circle for *NH, not here.*

**Say:** You should have darkened the circle under the first answer choice, 2. Nine invitations take away seven invitations equals two invitations. The correct answer is two.

**Say:** Now place your marker under the next row. This is Sample D. Listen carefully. You are asked to add eight and three. Use the scratch paper to work the problem. Then, darken the circle for the correct answer. If the correct answer is not given, darken the circle for *NH, not here.*

**Say:** You should have darkened the circle under the first number, 11. Eight plus three equals 11. The correct answer is 11.

**Say:** Now you will add or subtract more numbers in math problems you hear or read. Listen carefully to each problem. Then, darken the circle for the correct answer. If the correct answer is not given, darken the circle for *NH, not here.* If no choices are given, write the answer on the lines. Place your marker under the row for number 22.

**Say:**

22. Anton baked six square crackers on one cookie sheet. He baked five round crackers on another cookie sheet. How many crackers did Anton bake altogether? Write the number that tells how many crackers Anton baked altogether.

23. Place your marker under the next row for number 23. Misha saw fifteen butterflies on one bush. Then, he saw four butterflies on another bush. How many butterflies did he see altogether? Darken the circle under the number that tells how many butterflies Misha saw altogether.

24. Place your marker under the last row on the page. Pablo works at an animal shelter. He fed thirty-three dogs. Then, he fed twelve cats. How many dogs and cats did he feed altogether? Darken the circle under the number that tells how many dogs and cats Pablo fed altogether.

**Say:** Now turn to page 68. Now we will continue the test. Place your marker under the first row for number 25.

**Say:**

25. Listen carefully. Gabby and her family went camping. Gabby saw eight raccoons the first night. Her brother only saw six raccoons. How many more raccoons did Gabby see than her brother? Write the number that tells how many more raccoons Gabby saw than her brother.

26. Place your marker under the next row for number 26. There are fifteen people who play the trumpet in the school band. There are eight people who play the drums. How many more people play the trumpet than the drums? Darken the circle under the number that tells how many more people play the trumpet than the drums.

27. Place your marker under the next row for number 27. Claire went to the beach. She collected twenty-six shells. She put three of the shells back into the water because they were broken. How many shells did she have left? Darken the circle under the number that tells how many shells Claire has left.

28. Place your marker under the row for number 28. Mia took twenty-four balloons to school to share with her class. She gave out twenty balloons. How many balloons does she have left? Darken the circle under the number that tells how many balloons are left.

29. Place your marker under the last row on the page. The bus took fifty-seven children to school Monday morning. Only forty-five children rode the bus home Monday afternoon. How many children did not ride the bus home? Darken the circle under the number that tells how many children did not ride the bus home.

**Say:** Now look at page 69. In this part of the test you will add or subtract numbers. Do numbers 30 through 39 on your own. Read each problem carefully. Work the problem on the scratch paper. Then, darken the circle for the correct answer. If the correct answer is not given, darken the circle for *NH, not here.* If no choices are given, write your answer on the lines. You may now begin.

**Answers: Pages 63–69**
**Sample A:** 9, **Sample B:** 28, **1.** 2, **2.** 43, 13, **3.** 57, **4.** 25, **5.** 9 − 5 = 4, **6.** The fourth circle should be darkened., **7.** The second circle should be darkened., **8.** The first circle should be darkened., **9.** 50, **10.** The first circle should be darkened., **11.** The second circle should be darkened., **12.** The third circle should be darkened., **13.** 3, **14.** The first circle should be darkened., **15.** red, **16.** The second circle should be darkened., **17.** 19, **18.** The fourth circle should be darkened., **19.** 4 + 2 =, **20.** 15, **21.** The second circle should be darkened., **Sample C:** 2, **Sample D:** 11, **22.** 11, **23.** 19, **24.** 45, **25.** 2, **26.** 7, **27.** NH, **28.** 4, **29.** 12, **30.** 11, **31.** 14, **32.** 69, **33.** NH, **34.** 92, **35.** 0, **36.** 8, **37.** 52, **38.** 60, **39.** 504

# Unit 7

**Say:** Turn to page 70. In this lesson, you will practice choosing words or groups of words that best complete sentences. Listen carefully. I will read part of a sentence. The last word in the sentence is missing. Then, I will say the three words that are written on the lesson on page 70. You should listen for key words in each sentence. Then, read each answer choice to yourself. Decide which answer choice makes the most sense in the sentence. Now place your marker under Sample A. In Sample A, you see the words *flute*, *fiddle*, and *violet*. Now listen carefully. Brooke plays the violin. Another name for a violin is a—*flute … fiddle … violet*. Darken the circle beside the word that best completes the sentence.

**Say:** You should have darkened the circle next to the word *fiddle*. The key word in the sentence is *violin*. Another name for a violin is a fiddle. A flute is a musical instrument, but it is different from a violin. A violet is a flower.

**Say:** Now you will practice choosing more words that best complete sentences. Place your marker under number 1. Do numbers 1 through 12 just as you did Sample A. Listen carefully to the sentences and the three answer choices. Then, darken the circle beside the word or words that best complete the sentence.

**Say:**

1. We don't want anything to *harm* our new puppy. To harm means to—*help … heal … hurt*.

2. Place your marker under the next group of words. I'd like to *discover* some treasure. To discover something is to—*hide it … find it … bury it*.

3. Place your marker under the next group of words. Ava sat under a *clump* of trees. Another name for clump is—*limp … bunch … shade*.

4. Place your marker under the next group of words. Keesha *rescued* the baby bird. To rescue is to—*save … wash … feed*.

5. Place your marker under the next group of words. That shirt might *fade* in the wash. To fade is to—*get lighter … get darker … get smaller*.

6. Move to the top of the next column. Place your marker under the first group of words. Rodrigo gave Darla a birthday *gift*. Another name for gift is—*box … present … cake*.

7. Place your marker under the next group of words. We had to *pause* for a moment and rest. To pause is to—*wait … sleep … hurry*.

8. Place your marker under the next group of words. Kenji *aimed* the beanbag at the bucket. To aim is to—*clap … mark … point*.

9. Place your marker under the next group of words. Cheng fished in the *stream*. Another name for stream is—*creek … sea … pond*.

10. Place your marker under the next group of words. Dad *repaired* our toaster. To repair something is to—*replace it … fix it … return it*.

11. Place your marker under the next group of words. Your book is *below* the table. Another word for below is—*over … above … under*.

12. Place your marker under the last group of words. The sad story made us *weep*. To weep is to—*yell … laugh … cry*.

## Answers: Page 70
**Sample A:** fiddle, **1.** hurt, **2.** find it, **3.** bunch, **4.** save, **5.** get lighter, **6.** present, **7.** wait, **8.** point, **9.** creek, **10.** fix it, **11.** under, **12.** cry

## Page 71
**Say:** Turn to page 71. In this lesson you will practice choosing pictures that best answer questions. Listen carefully. I will read a story. Then, I will ask a question about the story. You will choose the picture that best answers the question. As you listen to the story, you should form a picture of the story in your mind. Then, choose the picture that comes closest to the picture in your mind.

Place your marker under the pictures in the first row. This is Sample A. Look at the pictures. Listen carefully. Every morning before school, Lita eats a good breakfast. After breakfast she always brushes her teeth. Next, she dresses and combs her hair. Then, she is ready to walk to the bus stop. What is the second thing Lita does before she leaves for school?—*Combs her hair … Eats breakfast … Brushes her teeth*?

**Say:** You should have darkened the circle under the third picture, the one that shows Lita brushing her teeth. The second thing Lita does before she goes to school is brush her teeth. First, she eats breakfast. Second, she brushes her teeth. Third, she dresses and combs her hair.

**Say:** Now you will practice choosing more pictures that best answer questions. Put your marker under number 1. Do numbers 1 through 7 just as you did Sample A. Study the pictures, and listen carefully to the story and the question. Then, darken the circle under the correct answer.

**Say:** Listen to this story. There are two questions. Mr. Sloop's class put on a talent show. The students helped with the show. Marcia and Tom made the scenery. Sam played the trumpet. Jody did a tap dance. Marty and Kim sang a song.

1. In the talent show Sam played—*a drum … a trumpet … a whistle*.

2. What is something another student could do in the talent show?—*Play a flute … Read a book … Jump rope*?

**Say:** Move your marker under number 3. Listen to this story. There is one question. Kyle's father is a baker. He owns his own bakery. Kyle visits the bakery. He likes the smell of fresh-baked goods.

3. Which of these could you buy in a bakery?—*An apple … An ice-cream cone …Bread*?

**Say:** Move your marker under number 4. Listen to this poem. There is one question.

If I could, you know I would,

Sail the ocean blue.

I'd have a big adventure,

And meet a pirate, too.

4. How will the author of the poem travel on the ocean?—*On a ship … In an airplane … In a truck*?

**Say:** Move your marker under number 5. Listen to this riddle. There is one question. I am sharp. My job is to cut hair. I can also be used to cut flowers and paper.

5. What am I?—*Scissors …Pencil …Comb*?

**Say:** Move your marker under number 6. Ella made a Mother's Day card for her stepmother. In the middle, she drew three roses. Above the roses, she drew a butterfly. Under the roses, she drew a bow. On top, she wrote "To Mother."

6. Darken the circle under the picture of Ella's finished card.

**Say:** Move your marker under number 7. Listen to this story. There is one question. In the fall Juan and Maria like to help their father. When the leaves have fallen from the trees, it is time for the family to start working.

7. How do Juan and Maria help their father in the fall? Do they—*rake leaves … shovel snow … water the garden*?

---

**Answers: Page 71**
**Sample A:** picture of girl brushing teeth, **1.** trumpet, **2.** girl playing flute, **3.** loaf of bread, **4.** ship, **5.** scissors, **6.** the middle card, **7.** children raking leaves

## Page 72

**Say:** Turn to page 72. In this lesson you will practice choosing words that best answer questions about stories that you hear. Listen carefully. I will read a story. Then, I will ask a question about the story. You will darken the circle beside the word or words that best answer the question. As you listen to the story, form a picture of the story in your mind. Listen carefully for details given in the story. Now place your marker under the words in the first row. This is Sample A. Listen carefully. Fidel went to the store. He bought paints and crayons for his art project. He also bought a book to read to his little sister. What will Fidel and his sister do?—*draw a picture … read a book … paint a picture*. Darken the circle beside the correct answer.

**Say:** You should have darkened the circle beside the second answer, read a book. The story tells you that Fidel bought a book to read to his sister. He bought crayons and paint for his art project.

**Say:** Now you will practice choosing more words that best answer questions about stories that you hear. Put your marker under number 1. Do numbers 1 through 9 just as you did Sample A. Listen to the story and the question. Then, darken the circle beside the correct answer.

**Say:** Listen as I read this story. You will answer two questions. Keiko has just lost her tooth. She is happy it fell out. It had been loose for seven days. Now she can eat without feeling any pain.

1. Keiko lost her tooth—*today … seven days ago … two weeks ago*.

2. Now it will be easier for Keiko to—*smile … talk … eat*.

**Say:** Now put your marker on number 3. You will answer two questions. Listen as I read this poem:

The animals lined up two by two

Today was a special parade at the zoo!

The giraffes so tall,

The ferrets so small,

And the elephants, of course, were the biggest of all.

3. Why were the animals lined up?—*It was raining. … There was a parade. … They were on their way to Africa*.

4. Which animals were tall?—*elephants … ferrets … giraffes.*

**Say:** Now put your marker under number 5. Listen as I read this story. You will answer two questions. The word *dinosaur* means "terrible lizard." These creatures roamed Earth many millions of years ago. Some were as small as chickens. Others were much larger than elephants. We learn about dinosaurs from the things they left behind. No people were living then to tell us about dinosaurs.

5. How small were some dinosaurs?—*as small as bees … as small as teacups … as small as chickens.*

6. How do we learn about dinosaurs?—*from the things they left behind … from the people who were living then … from animals today.*

**Say:** Now put your marker under number 7. Listen as I read these directions for making a breakfast dish. You will answer two questions about the directions.

1. First, take the eggs, bread, and milk out of the refrigerator.
2. Next, break the eggs, and use a fork to mix them with milk.
3. Then, put the bread into the bowl. Turn it over.
4. Finally, cook the bread in a pan on the stove.
5. When your French toast is ready, enjoy your breakfast!

**Say:**

7. These directions tell you how to make—*biscuits … French toast … cereal.*

8. What should you do after you mix the milk and eggs in the bowl?—*add the bread … put it on the stove … stir in some butter.*

**Say:** Now put your marker on number 9. Listen as I read this story. You will answer one question.

Courtney's mom planned a picnic for her family. She packed a basket with sandwiches, potato salad, fruit, and cookies. She told everyone in the family to be ready at noon on Saturday. But she didn't tell them where they would go for the picnic.

9. Who planned the picnic?—*Courtney … Courtney's mom … Courtney's whole family.*

**Answers: Page 72**
**Sample A:** read a book, **1.** today, **2.** eat, **3.** There was a parade., **4.** giraffes, **5.** as small as chickens, **6.** from the things they left behind, **7.** French toast, **8.** add the bread, **9.** Courtney's mom

## Test: Pages 73–75

**Say:** Turn to the Unit 7 Test on page 73. In this test you will use the listening skills we have practiced in this unit. This test is divided into three parts. For each part there is a sample exercise. We will work each sample together. Look at Sample A. In this part of the test, you will choose the word or words that best complete sentences. I will read part of a sentence and three words. You will find the word or words that best complete the sentence. Listen carefully. We had to *speak very quietly* in the library. To speak very quietly is to—*shout … laugh … whisper.* Darken the circle beside the correct answer.

**Say:** You should have darkened the circle beside the word *whisper* because to speak very quietly is to *whisper.*

**Say:** Now you will choose more words that best complete sentences. Put your marker on number 1. Do numbers 1 through 12 just as you did Sample A. Listen carefully to the sentence and the three answer choices. Then, darken the circle beside the correct answer.

**Say:**

1. My uncle has a *cabin* at the lake. A cabin is a—*shed … boat … small house.*
2. Put your marker under the next row of words. Jose has to *prepare* for his part in the play. To prepare is to—*calm down … leave … get ready.*
3. Put your marker under the next row of words. Zoe saw a *bug* on a leaf. Another name for bug is—*insect … igloo … pet.*
4. Put your marker under the next row of words. This instrument makes a sound when you *strike* it. To strike is to—*hit … smooth … clean.*
5. Put your marker under the next row of words. Our family took a *vacation* to the Grand Canyon. Another name for vacation is—*illness … trip … excuse.*
6. Put your marker under the next row of words. Su Ling was *tardy* this morning. To be tardy is to be—*present … late … early.*
7. Put your marker on number 7 at the top of the next column. That happened *the day before today.* The day before today is called—*tomorrow … tonight … yesterday.*
8. Put your marker under the next row of words. My mom met a *pleasant* lady who gave us directions. Pleasant means—*nice … rude … poor.*

9. Put your marker under the next row of words. Katy found an unusual rock. If something is *unusual*, it is—*not common … square … normal*.

10. Put your marker under the next row of words. The knight was *brave* as he fought the dragon. Brave means—*not afraid … not angry … not smart*.

11. Put your marker under the next row of words. The weather forecaster said clouds might *appear* today. To appear is to—*go away … be seen … get faster*.

12. Put your marker under the last row of words. We took a walk through the *woods* and saw many animals and trees. Another word for woods is—*ocean … desert … forest*.

**Say:** Turn to page 74. In this part of the test, you will choose pictures that best answer questions. I will read a story and then ask a question. You will choose the picture that best answers the question. Place your marker under Sample B. Look at the pictures. Listen carefully. Young children should never play with matches. My brother Tommy struck a match. He dropped it when it got hot. The burning match fell onto the chair. Darken the circle under the picture that shows what probably happened next.

**Say:** You should have darkened the circle under the first picture that shows the burning chair. When a burning match is dropped onto a chair, the chair will burn.

**Say:** Now you will choose more pictures that best answer questions about stories that you hear. Put your marker on number 13. Do numbers 13 through 21 just as you did Sample B. Study the pictures, and listen carefully to each story and question. Then, darken the circle under the correct answer.

**Say:**

13. Fatima was helping her aunt make a quilt. Fatima cut four squares and three circles from each piece of cloth. Darken the circle under the picture that shows how Fatima cut each piece of cloth.

14. Move your marker under number 14. Miko turned on the water in the tub to take a bath. Then, the telephone rang, and Miko answered it. She talked to her friend for an hour and forgot about the water in the tub. Darken the circle under the picture that shows what probably happened next.

15. Move your marker under number 15. Amy was learning a new dance. Her teacher told her to start by putting her arms down by her sides and stand with her feet apart. Darken the circle under the picture of Amy starting her new dance.

**Say:** Now place your marker under number 16. Listen to this story. There is one question. Diego's grandmother gave him a box with a new pet in it. When Diego looked in the box, he saw long ears and a short, fluffy tail.

16. What pet did Diego receive?—*A rabbit … A mouse … A dog*?

**Say:** Now place your marker at the top of the second column under number 17. Listen to this story. There is one question. Mr. Sakata told his class, "This week you will choose a book from the school library to read. The book must tell a story. Then, you will write a report about your book."

17. What must each student do first to write the book report?—*Choose a book … Read a report … Watch TV*?

**Say:** Now place your marker under number 18. Listen to this story. There is one question. Mr. Jordan made a delicious strawberry pie. First, he chopped the strawberries. Then, he mixed the dough for the crust. Finally, he rolled the dough flat.

18. What did Mr. Jordan do second? Did he—*chop strawberries … roll the dough … mix the dough for the crust*?

**Say:** Now place your marker under number 19. Listen to this story. There are two questions. No one had lived in the old house on Roland Road for more than ten years. It was very scary-looking. One night Paul and his friend Steve visited the house. Just as they opened the front door, something small and furry brushed against their legs. The boys decided to explore the house some other day and they ran home.

19. Darken the circle under the picture that shows the house on Roland Road.

20. Move your marker under number 20. What probably brushed by the boys at the house? Was it—*a cat … a turtle … a parrot*?

**Say:** Move your marker under number 21. Listen to this story. Alex baked muffins for the school bake sale. He measured and mixed the ingredients. Then, he poured the batter into a pan and put the pan into the oven to bake.

21. Darken the circle under the picture that shows the baking pan Alex used.

**Say:** Now go to page 75. In this part of the test, you will choose words that best answer questions about stories that you hear. I will read a story and then ask a question. You will choose the best answer to the question. Now look at Sample C. Listen carefully. Nancy's mom took her to a children's museum. There Nancy pretended to be a firefighter. She put on a big coat, boots, and a hat. She also watched a video about bats and built a skyscraper with blocks. Nancy's mom took her to a—*store … museum … park.* Darken the circle beside the correct answer.

**Say:** You should have darkened the circle beside the word *museum*, because the first sentence of the story says that Nancy's mom took her to the children's museum.

**Say:** Now you will choose more words that best answer questions about stories that you hear. Put your marker under number 22. Do numbers 22 through 33 just as you did Sample C. Listen carefully to the story and question. Then, darken the circle beside the correct answer.

**Say:** Listen as I read these directions. You will answer two questions.

1. First, take the kite out of the package.
2. Second, insert the wooden pieces into the back of the kite.
3. Next, attach the end of a ball of string to the center of the kite.
4. Finally, make a kite's tail from pieces of cloth and attach it to the kite.
5. If you'd like, you can paint or decorate your kite.

**Say:**

22. The reason wooden pieces are attached to the kite is so that—*the kite can fly … the kite won't blow away … you can decorate the kite.*

23. To make the kite fly, you do not have to—*attach some string … insert wooden pieces … paint the kite.*

**Say:** Now put your marker on number 24. Listen as I read this story. You will answer two questions. Rod helps his family with the store every day. Before going to school, Rod sweeps the store. After school, Rod does his homework. Then, he takes out the trash. When it is time to close the store, Rod makes sure all the lights are turned out.

24. Before he goes to school, Rod helps by—*sweeping the store … taking out the trash … turning out all the lights.*

25. Rod helps close the store by—*doing his homework … taking out the trash … turning out all the lights.*

**Say:** Now put your marker on number 26. You will answer two questions. Water is one of the most valuable things on Earth. There are many simple ways to save water. One is to take showers instead of baths. Showers use much less water, and get you just as clean! You can also save water when you are washing your hands and brushing your teeth. Don't let the water run while you are soaping up your hands or brushing your teeth. Turn on the water just when you need it to rinse. Doing simple things like these helps save water and keep the Earth green.

26. One thing that does not help save water is—*taking a shower … catching rainwater … taking a bath.*

27. When washing your hands, you should turn on the water only to—*soap up your hands … rinse … take a bath.*

**Say:** Now put your marker on number 28 at the top of the next column. Listen carefully as I read the poem. You will answer two questions.

"Good gracious me!" said Jake.

When he opened his backpack,

Out came his snake!

28. What came out of Jake's backpack?—*his frog … his snake … his homework.*

29. How did Jake feel when he saw it?—*surprised … tired … sad.*

**Say:** Now put your marker on number 30. Listen carefully as I read this story. You will answer two questions. Ms. Jackson's class was doing a science experiment. She divided the class into groups and gave each person a job. "In this group, Michiko will pass out the materials," Ms. Jackson said. "Jamal will be the recorder. Scott will be in charge of cleanup. Jenna will be the leader."

30. Ms. Jackson's class was—*practicing a play … running a race … doing a science experiment.*

31. Who will be the leader?—*Michiko … Jenna …. Jamal.*

**Say:** Now put your marker on number 32. Listen as I read this story. You will answer two questions. Mr. Díaz packed all the gear for the family's camping trip. He packed the tent and a cooler with all the food. He packed lanterns, flashlights, and bug spray. At the campsite, they set up the tent. They cooked a meal over the fire. Only when it was time to go to bed did the Díaz family discover that Mr. Díaz had forgotten to pack something.

32. Mr. Díaz forgot to pack the family's—*sleeping bags … radio … flashlights.*

33. A good title for this story would be—*"How to Go Camping" … "The Díaz Family's Problem" … "Fun with Flashlights."*

**Answers: Pages 73–75**
Sample A: whisper, **1.** small house, **2.** get ready,
**3.** insect, **4.** hit, **5.** trip, **6.** late, **7.** yesterday, **8.** nice,
**9.** not common, **10.** not afraid, **11.** be seen,
**12.** forest, **Sample B:** The first circle should be
darkened., **13.** The second circle should be
darkened., **14.** The third circle should be darkened.,
**15.** The second circle should be darkened., **16.** The
first circle should be darkened., **17.** The first circle
should be darkened., **18.** The third circle should be
darkened., **19.** The first circle should be darkened.,
**20.** The first circle should be darkened., **21.** The first
circle should be darkened., **Sample C:** museum,
**22.** the kite can fly, **23.** paint the kite, **24.** sweeping
the store, **25.** turning out all the lights, **26.** taking a
bath, **27.** rinse, **28.** his snake, **29.** surprised,
**30.** doing a science experiment, **31.** Jenna,
**32.** sleeping bags, **33.** "The Díaz Family's Problem"

# Unit 8

## Pages 76

**Say:** Turn to page 76. In this lesson you will practice choosing pictures that answer questions about stories you hear. When I read a story, you should listen very carefully. Look at the pictures for the story. Then, find the picture that answers the question about the story. Place your marker under the first row. This is Sample A. Now listen carefully. It was Saturday, and it was raining. Mei could not go out to play with her friends. After she ate lunch, Mei told her mother, "I have nothing to do. What can I do that's fun?" Her mother asked, "Why don't you watch TV?" But Mei said she didn't want to watch TV. Then, Mei's mother showed her a trunk filled with old clothes, purses, hats, and other things. Mei's mother said, "Here, use your imagination and have fun." Darken the circle for the picture that shows how Mei had fun on a rainy Saturday.

**Say:** You should have darkened the circle for the third picture. Mei dressed in some of the clothes and things she found in the trunk. She had fun playing dress-up and using her imagination.

**Say:** Now you will practice choosing more pictures that answer questions about stories you hear. Listen carefully to each story. Then, choose your answer from the pictures given for the story.

Now we will begin. Place your marker under the next row. Look at the pictures of the plates and the spoons and forks. Listen to this story.

**Say:**

1. Elena and Ricardo were helping their mother by setting the table for dinner. Elena placed the spoon and fork on either side of the plate. Ricardo crossed the spoon and fork and put them on the plate. Then, the spoon cried, "That's not right!," and it jumped off the plate. Darken the circle for the picture that shows something that could not happen.

2. Place your marker under the next row. Listen to this poem.

My Grandmother lives in the state of Maine.

When we go to visit her, we travel by _____.

Darken the circle for the picture that rhymes with the poem.

3. Place your marker under the next row. Look at the pictures of the animals. Frankie's father gave him a box with a new pet in it. When Frankie looked into the box, he saw short ears and a wagging tail. Darken the circle for the picture that shows Frankie's new pet.

4. Place your marker under the last row on the page. Mr. Henson was building a new doghouse for his dog, Grover. First, he sawed the wood into the pieces that he needed. Next, he nailed the pieces together to make the doghouse. Finally, he painted Grover's new doghouse. Darken the circle for the picture that shows what Mr. Henson did first.

## Answers: Page 76

Sample A: The third circle should be darkened.,
**1.** The third circle should be darkened., **2.** The second circle should be darkened., **3.** The second circle should be darkened., **4.** The first circle should be darkened.

## Pages 77–82

**Say:** Turn to page 77. In this lesson you will practice finding words and sentences that answer questions about stories you hear. When I read a story, you should listen very carefully. Look at the answer choices for the story. Then, find the one that best answers the question. Place your marker under the first row. Be sure to move your marker so you can see all the answer choices. This is Sample A. Look at the picture under the title "Julie's Trip to Mexico" while I read you a story about Julie. Now listen carefully. Julie's family is taking a boat trip to Mexico. She is keeping a journal about all the things she does on her trip. Which activity will not be in Julie's journal? Is it— *Swimming in the ocean … Shopping in the market at home…* or *Games we play on the ship*? Darken the circle beside the activity which will not be in Julie's journal.

**Say:** You should have darkened the circle for the second answer, *Shopping in the market at home.* This is the correct answer. This activity does not belong in Julie's journal because Julie is keeping a journal about things she does on her trip. This activity takes place at home, not on her trip.

**Say:** Place your marker under the next row. This is Sample B. This is what Julie wrote on one page of her journal. Read it silently to yourself as I read it aloud.

Shopping was fun.

Mother <u>buyed</u> me a hat.

Look at the underlined word. Did Julie use the right word? Should she write—*bought … buy …* or is the underlined word *Correct the way it is*? Darken the circle for the way Julie should write the underlined word.

**Say:** You should have darkened the circle for the first answer, *bought.* Julie should write *My mother bought me a hat.*

**Say:** Place your marker under the next row. This is Sample C. This is what Julie wrote on another page of her journal. Read it silently to yourself as I read it aloud.

We swam in the water.

And played in the waves.

We made sand castles.

Which group of words is not a complete sentence? Is it—*We swam in the water. … And played in the waves. …* or *We made sand castles.*? Darken the circle beside the words that do not make a complete sentence.

**Say:** You should have darkened the circle for the second answer, *And played in the waves.* These words do not make a complete sentence.

**Say:** Now turn to page 78. Now you will practice finding more words and sentences that answer questions about stories you hear. Listen carefully to each story. Then, choose your answer from the words and sentences given. Place your marker under the first row. Be sure to move your marker so you can see all the answer choices. Look at the picture under the title "Larry's Horse" while I read you a story about Larry. Then, you will answer some questions about this story. Now listen carefully.

**Say:**

1. Larry's teacher asked the class to write a story about their pets. Larry has a horse. He decided to write about the tricks his horse can do. Why is Larry writing a story? Is it—*to tell how to teach a horse tricks … to tell why he loves horses …* or *to tell a story about his pet*? Darken the circle for the answer that tells why Larry is writing a story.

2. Place your marker under the next row. Larry used these words in his story: *kiss, tricks,* and *hand.* He wanted to look them up in the dictionary to make sure they were spelled correctly. Darken the circle for the word that would be listed first in alphabetical (ABC) order in the dictionary.

**Say:** Look at the first part of Larry's story, under the title "My Smart Horse." Read it silently to yourself as I read it aloud.

My Smart Horse

My horse can do many tricks.

<u>He lifts his leg to my hand shake</u>.

He gives me a kiss with his nose.

My horse can also play hiding games.

**Say:** Now you will answer some questions. Place your marker under the next row for number 3. Be sure to move your marker so you can see all the answer choices.

3. Look at the underlined sentence that reads, *He lifts his leg to my hand shake.* Did Larry write the sentence correctly? Should he write—*He lifts his leg to hand shake my. … He lifts his leg to shake my hand. …* or is the sentence *Correct the way it is*? Darken the circle for the way Larry should write the sentence.

4. Place your marker under the last row on the page. Larry wanted to describe his horse. Would he write—*My horse is brown and white. … I like to see my horse run. …* or *My horse comes when he sees me.*? Darken the circle for the sentence Larry will write to describe his horse.

**Say:** Now go to page 79. Now we will continue the lesson. Look at the rest of Larry's story at the top of the page. Listen to what Larry wrote next in his story. Read it silently to yourself as I read it aloud.

I <u>gived</u> my horse a treat after each trick.
  (1)

He <u>likes</u> carrots best.
  (2)

If I forget his treat, he shakes his head.

**Say:** Now place your marker under the first row.

5. Look at the underlined word, *gived*, with the number 1 under it. Did Larry use the right word? Should he write—*gave … give …* or is the word *Correct the way it is*? Darken the circle for the way Larry should write the underlined word.

6. Place your marker under the next row. Look at the underlined word, *likes*, with the number 2 under it. Did Larry use the right word? Should he write—*like … liked …* or is the word *Correct the way it is*? Darken the circle for the way Larry should write the underlined word.

**Say:** Now I will read you another story. Look at the picture under the title "Going Places." Now listen while I read you a story about Keisha. Keisha is writing a report about how people travel from place to place. She put a Table of Contents at the front of her report. Read it silently to yourself as I read it aloud. Chapter 1 is called "Over Tracks" and begins on page 6. Chapter 2 is called "Up in Air" and begins on page 21. Chapter 3 is called "On Land" and begins on page 38. Chapter 4 is called "By Water" and begins on page 50. Now place your marker under the next row.

**Say:**

7. Look at the Table of Contents. Would Keisha write about airplanes in Chapter 1, 2, or 3? Darken the circle for the chapter in which Keisha would write about airplanes.

8. Place your marker under the last row on the page. Look at the Table of Contents again. Would Keisha write about ships on page 21, page 38, or page 50? Darken the circle for the page on which Keisha would write about ships.

**Say:** Now turn to page 80. Now we will continue the lesson. Look at the title "Getting Around in the City." Listen to what Keisha wrote in her report. Read it silently to yourself as I read it aloud.

Getting Around in the City

Many people drive cars.

In large cities.

Some people ride in taxis.

Most people ride the bus.

**Say:** Now place your marker under the first row.

9. Which sentence is not a complete sentence? Is it—*Many people drive cars. … In large cities. …* or *Some people ride in taxis.*? Darken the circle for the group of words that is not a complete sentence.

10. Place your marker under the next row. Which sentence will Keisha write next? Will she write—*A few people might walk to work. … People work in a city. …* or *The city is noisy.*? Darken the circle for the sentence Keisha will write next.

**Say:** Now listen to what Keisha wrote next in her report. Read it silently to yourself as I read it aloud.

<u>We lives</u> in the city.
   (1)

<u>My father</u> rides a bus to work.
   (2)

It is too far for him to walk.

**Say:** Now place your marker under the next row.

11. Look at the underlined words with the number 1 under them. Did Keisha use the right words? Should she write—*We is living …We live …* or is the group of underlined words *Correct the way it is*? Darken the circle for the way Keisha should write the underlined words.

12. Place your marker under the last row on the page. Look at the underlined words with the number 2 under them. Did Keisha use the right words? Should she write—*My Father … my father …* or is the group of words *Correct the way it is*? Darken the circle for the way Keisha should write the group of underlined words.

**Say:** Now go to page 81. Now we will continue the lesson. Now I will read you another story. Look at the picture under the title "A Surprise for Father" while I read you a story about Rena. Rena is planning a birthday surprise for her father. She wants to write a poem for her father. She wants to write about all the special things they do together. Now place your marker under the first row.

**Say:**

13. What should Rena do before writing her poem? Should she—*bake her father a cake … make a list of things she does with her father …* or *read a book of poems*? Darken the circle that tells what Rena should do first.

14. Place your marker under the next row. What is this story about? Is it about—*a birthday party … a present Rena will give her father …* or *things Rena likes to do with her father*? Darken the circle that tells what the story is about.

**Say:** Listen to the poem Rena wrote. It is called "My Family." Read it silently to yourself as I read it aloud.

My Family

Together we have fun.

We laugh and we run.

We fish in the lake.

And Mother likes to bake.

Sometimes we go on hikes.

**Say:** Now place your marker under the next row.

15. Which sentence does not belong in the poem? Is it—*Together we have fun. … We fish in the lake. …* or *And Mother likes to bake.*? Darken the circle for the sentence that does not belong in the poem.

16. Now place your marker under the last row on the page. Which sentence will Rena probably write next? Will she write—*And then we ride our bikes. … I am happy. …* or *You are fun.*? Darken the circle for the sentence that Rena will probably write next.

**Say:** Now turn to page 82. Now we will continue the lesson. Listen to the rest of the story about Rena. When Rena finished the poem, she wrote a letter at the bottom of her poem. Read the letter silently to yourself as I read it aloud.

Dear Father,
       (1)
Are you having a fun birthday
                        (2)
I wanted to make it special.
    (3)
I love you.
Your daughter,
Rena

**Say:** Now place your marker under the next row.

17. Look at the underlined words with the number 1 under them. How should Rena write these words? Should she write—*Dear father … dear Father …* or is the group of words *Correct the way it is*? Darken the circle for the way Rena should write the underlined words.

18. Place your marker under the next row. Look at the underlined word with the number 2 under it. Which punctuation mark should Rena write at the end of this sentence? Should she write—*a question mark … a period …* or *an exclamation point*? Darken the circle for the punctuation mark Rena should write after the underlined word.

19. Place your marker under the last row on the page. Look at the words with the number 3 under them. How should Rena write these words? Should she write—*I wants … I wanting …* or is the group of words *Correct the way it is*? Darken the circle for the way Rena should write the underlined words.

**Answers: Pages 77–82**
**Sample A:** Shopping in the market at home, **Sample B:** bought, **Sample C:** And played in the waves., **1.** to tell a story about his pet, **2.** hand, **3.** He lifts his leg to shake my hand., **4.** My horse is brown and white., **5.** give, **6.** Correct the way it is, **7.** 2, **8.** 50, **9.** In large cities., **10.** A few people might walk to work., **11.** We live, **12.** Correct the way it is, **13.** make a list of things she does with her father, **14.** a present Rena will give her father, **15.** And Mother likes to bake., **16.** And then we ride our bikes., **17.** Correct the way it is, **18.** birthday?, **19.** Correct the way it is

## Page 83

**Say:** Turn to page 83. In this lesson you will practice finding words that are not spelled correctly.

Listen carefully. I will read a sentence. Three of the words will be listed in the row. When I read a sentence, you should look at each word. Then, find the word that is not spelled correctly.

Place your marker under the first row. This is Sample A. Now listen carefully to this sentence. *I wint (went) along for the ride.* Darken the circle next to the word that is not spelled correctly.

**Say:** You should have darkened the circle for the first word, *wint. Went* is the word that is not spelled correctly. *Went* should have an *e* where the *i* is.

**Say:** Now you will practice choosing more words that are not spelled correctly. Look at the words silently as I read the sentence aloud. Darken the circle for the word that is not spelled correctly. Now place your marker under the next row.

**Say:**

1. *Did you see the cake I bakt (baked)?* Darken the circle next to the word that is not spelled correctly.

2. Place your marker under the next row. *He wus (was) eating an apple.* Darken the circle next to the word that is not spelled correctly.

3. Place your marker under the next row. *Tony walkt (walked) to the store by himself.* Darken the circle next to the word that is not spelled correctly.

4. Place your marker under the next row. Listen to this sentence. *The two babies playd (played) quietly.* Darken the circle next to the word that is not spelled correctly.

5. Place your marker under the next row. *Alberto had a party at skool (school) today.* Darken the circle next to the word that is not spelled correctly.

**Say:** Now look at the top of the page. Find the next column. Place your marker under the first row.

6. *Pleaze (please) pass the milk.* Darken the circle next to the word that is not spelled correctly.

7. Place your marker under the next row. *I can cros (cross) the street now.* Darken the circle next to the word that is not spelled correctly.

8. Place your marker under the next row. *Those boyes (boys) joined the baseball team.* Darken the circle next to the word that is not spelled correctly.

9. Place your marker under the next row. *The frog sat on the gren (green) grass.* Darken the circle next to the word that is not spelled correctly.

10. Place your marker under the next row. *It is Raúl's turn to wash dishs (dishes).* Darken the circle next to the word that is not spelled correctly.

11. Place your marker under the last row. Listen to this sentence. *Brian pickd (picked) these flowers.* Darken the circle next to the word that is not spelled correctly.

**Answers: Page 83**
**Sample A:** wint, **1.** bakt, **2.** wus, **3.** walkt, **4.** playd, **5.** skool, **6.** Pleaze, **7.** cros, **8.** boyes, **9.** gren, **10.** dishs, **11.** pickd

**Test: Pages 84–91**
**Say:** Turn to the Unit 8 Test on page 84. In the first part of the test you will choose pictures that answer questions about stories you hear. Place your marker under the first row. This is Sample A. Now listen carefully. Everyone said that the old house on Roland Road was haunted. No one had lived there for more than ten years. The house and yard were no longer cared for. Darken the circle for the picture that shows how the house probably looked.

**Say:** You should have darkened the circle for the second picture. The second picture shows a house that needs to be fixed and bushes that need to be trimmed.

**Say:** Now you will choose more pictures that answer questions about stories you hear. Listen carefully to each story. Then, choose your answer from the pictures given in the row. Place your marker under the next row.

**Say:**

1. Inez and Isabela are twins. Even though they look alike, they are very different. They like to do different things. They wear their hair the same way, but they always dress differently. Darken the circle for the picture that shows Inez and Isabela.

2. Place your marker under the next row. Chris and his family went to the lake. They saw a family of bears swimming across the lake. Then, the bears joined Chris and his family at the picnic table for lunch. Later, Chris offered to clean up the mess at the picnic table. Darken the circle for the picture that shows something that could not happen.

3. Place your marker under the next row. Listen to this poem.

While we were walking by the lake,

We saw a black and yellow _____.

Darken the circle for the picture that will rhyme with the poem.

4. Place your marker under the last row on the page. Gloria was very busy on Saturday. She made her bed and then washed the dishes. When she was done, she went to her room to work on some homework. Darken the circle for the picture that shows what Gloria did first.

**Say:** Now go to page 85. In the next part of the test I will ask you questions about stories you hear. Listen carefully to the story and questions. Then, choose your answer from the words and sentences given. Place your marker under the first row. Be sure to move your marker so you can see all the answer choices. This is Sample B. Look at the picture under the title "Takshi's Friend" while I read you a story about Takshi.

**Say:** Now listen carefully. Takshi is writing a letter to a pen pal. A pen pal is a person that lives far away and someone the letter writer does not know. They write letters to each other. Takshi is telling the pen pal about himself. Which description will not be in Takshi's letter? Is it—*What Takshi looks like … Why Takshi wants a pen pal …* or *Games Takshi likes to play*? Darken the circle beside the description that will not be in Takshi's letter.

**Say:** You should have darkened the circle for the second answer, *Why Takshi wants a pen pal*. The second answer does not describe Takshi.

**Say:** Place your marker under the next row. This is Sample C. Listen carefully to the beginning of Takshi's letter. Read it silently to yourself as I read it aloud.

Dear Peter,

I want to tell you about me.

I am in the first grade.

I like to play baseball.

Every day after school.

**Say:** Which group of words is not a complete sentence? Is it—*I am in the first grade. … I like to play baseball. …* or *Every day after school.*? Darken the circle beside the words that do not make a complete sentence.

**Say:** You should have darkened the circle for the last group of words, Every day after school. These words do not make a complete sentence.

**Say:** Now place your marker under the next row. This is Sample D. Listen to the last part of Takshi's letter. Read it silently to yourself as I read it aloud.

Will you underline{writing} soon?

I want to know more about you.

Your friend,

Takshi

Look at the underlined word. Did Takshi use the right word? Should it be—*write … writes …* or is the underlined word *Correct the way it is*? Darken the circle for the way Takshi should write the underlined word.

**Say:** You should have darkened the circle for the first word, *write*. The sentence should read, *Will you write soon?*

**Say:** Now turn to page 86. Now we will continue the test. You will find more words and sentences that answer questions about stories you hear. Listen carefully to each story. Then, choose your answer from the words and sentences given. Look at the picture under the title "Pat's Science Project," while I read you a story about Pat. Pat is going to make a project for the school's science fair. She is going to tell how seeds move from place to place. Now place your marker under the first row. Be sure to move your marker so you can see all the answer choices.

**Say:**

5. What should Pat do before writing her science report? Should she—*list ways seeds move … plant some seeds …* or *glue seeds to paper*? Darken the circle that tells what Pat should do first.

6. Place your marker under the next row. What should Pat do to find more information about how seeds move? Should she—*buy seeds from a store … find a library book about seeds …* or *go to a park*? Darken the circle for what Pat should do to find more information about how seeds move.

**Say:** Listen to Pat's science report, titled "Animals Help Move Seeds." Read it silently to yourself as I read it aloud.

Animals Help Move Seeds

Some animals help move seeds.

Birds pick up seeds to eat.

They may underline{dropping} the seeds as they fly.

I have a new dog.

The seeds grow where they fall on the ground.

**Say:** Now go to page 87. Place your marker under the first row.

7. Look at the underlined word. How should Pat write this word? Should she write—*drops … drop …* or is the underlined word *Correct the way it is*? Darken the circle for the way Pat should write the underlined word.

8. Place your marker under the next row on the page. Which sentence does not belong in the story? Is it—*Some animals help move seeds. … Birds pick up seeds to eat. …* or *I have a new dog.*? Darken the circle for the sentence that does not belong in the story.

**Say:** Now place your marker under the next row. Listen to the rest of Pat's science report. Read it silently to yourself as I read it aloud.

Some seeds stick to the fur of animals.

They underline{dont} fall off easily.

The ends of the seeds are turned up.

**Say:** Now place your marker under the next row.

9. Look at the underlined word. How should Pat write this word? Should she write—*don't … do'nt …* or is the underlined word *Correct the way it is*? Darken the circle for the way Pat should write the underlined word.

10. Place your marker under the next row. Pat wants to describe what the seed looks like. Which sentence is the best way for Pat to tell what the seed looks like? Should she write—*The seed ends look sharp and look like a fishhook. … The seed ends look sharp and like a fishhook. …* or *The seed ends look like a sharp fishhook.*? Darken the circle for the sentence that is the best way for Pat to tell what the seed looks like.

**Say:**

11. Place your marker under the last row on the page. Pat used these words in her story: *stick*, *seeds*, and *sharp*. She wanted to look them up in the dictionary to make sure they were spelled correctly. Darken the circle for the word that would be listed first in alphabetical (ABC) order in the dictionary.

**Say:** Now turn to page 88. I will read you another story. Look at the picture under the title "Mr. Lee's New Car," while I read you a story about Mr. Lee. Mr. Lee is going to sell his car. He wants to buy a new car. He is making a list of things he will look for in his new car. Now place your marker under the first row.

**Say:**

12. What should Mr. Lee do to find more information about how safe a car is? Should he—*talk to a car salesperson … drive a car …* or *look under a car*? Darken the circle for what Mr. Lee should do to find more information about how safe a car is.

13. Place your marker under the last row on the page. Which will not be on Mr. Lee's list? Will it be—*a red car … a safe car …* or *wash the car*? Darken the circle for what will not be on Mr. Lee's list.

**Say:** Now go to page 89. Place your marker under the first row, which shows Mr. Lee's list, "Car Safety." Listen to what Mr. Lee wrote on his list. Read it silently to yourself as I read it aloud.

Car Safety

The car should be very safe. It needs seat belts in the front and the back. It must have new tires. The horn should honk. Very loudly for people to hear.

**Say:** Now place your marker under the next row.

14. Mr. Lee wants to tell more about how the car should look. Should he write—*The car will have two doors. … I want a car I saw at the store. …* or *It should be a new car.*? Darken the circle for the words that tell how Mr. Lee's car will look.

15. Place your marker under the last row on the page. Which group of words is not a complete sentence? Is it—*The car should be very safe. … It must have new tires. …* or *Very loudly for people to hear.*? Darken the circle beside the words that do not make a complete sentence.

**Say:** Now turn to page 90. Now listen to the rest of the story about Mr. Lee. Mr. Lee needs to sell his old car before he buys the new one. He wrote a description of his car to put in the newspaper. This is what he wrote. Read it silently to yourself as I read it aloud.

Car for Sale

I have a car for sale.
(1)

It is in very good shape.

I need to sell it before Thursday, june 28.
(2)

**Say:** Now place your marker under the next row.

16. Look at the underlined word with the number 1 under it. Did Mr. Lee use the right word? Should he write—*had … has …* or is it *Correct the way it is*? Darken the circle for the way the underlined word should be written.

17. Place your marker under the next row. Look at the underlined words with the number 2 under them. How should the words be written? Should they be written—*thursday, june 28 … Thursday, June 28 …* or is the group of words *Correct the way it is*? Darken the circle for the way the underlined words should be written.

18. Place your marker under the last row on the page. Which sentence will Mr. Lee probably write next? Will he write—*Please call to find out more. … The car is sold. …* or *I want to buy a blue car.*? Darken the circle for the sentence Mr. Lee will probably write next.

**Say:** Now go to page 91. In the last part of the test you will find words that are not spelled correctly. Listen carefully. I will read a sentence. Three of the words are listed as the answer choices. Find the word that is not spelled correctly. Now place your marker under the first row. This is Sample E. *The play was overe (over) at four o'clock.* Darken the circle next to the word that is not spelled correctly.

**Say:** You should have darkened the circle for the second word, *overe*. The word *over* is not spelled with an e at the end.

**Say:** Now you will find more words that are not spelled correctly. Place your marker under the next row.

19. *The pretty (pretty) pink present is for Grandmother.* Darken the circle next to the word that is not spelled correctly.

20. Place your marker under the next row. *Liz told a funny storie (story).* Darken the circle next to the word that is not spelled correctly.

21. Place your marker under the next row. Listen to this sentence. *This is the ende (end) of the line.* Darken the circle next to the word that is not spelled correctly.

22. Place your marker under the next row. *The boys splashd (splashed) in the water.* Darken the circle next to the word that is not spelled correctly.

23. Place your marker under the next row. *Max bought two brushs (brushes).* Darken the circle next to the word that is not spelled correctly.

**Say:** Now look at the top of the next column. Place your marker under the first row.

24. *I didn't mean what I sed (said).* Darken the circle next to the word that is not spelled correctly.

25. Place your marker under the next row. *The pond is filld (filled) with fish.* Darken the circle next to the word that is not spelled correctly.

26. Place your marker under the next row. *Your fase (face) has dirt on it.* Darken the circle next to the word that is not spelled correctly.

27. Place your marker under the next row. *Put your toyes (toys) away in your room.* Darken the circle next to the word that is not spelled correctly.

28. Place your marker under the next row. *Mother parkt (parked) close to the house.* Darken the circle next to the word that is not spelled correctly.

29. Place your marker under the last row. Listen to this sentence. *The snake livz (lives) under the rock.* Darken the circle next to the word that is not spelled correctly.

**Answers: Pages 84–91**
**Sample A:** The second circle should be darkened., **1.** The third circle should be darkened., **2.** The second circle should be darkened., **3.** The third circle should be darkened., **4.** The first circle should be darkened., **Sample B:** Why Takshi wants a pen pal, **Sample C:** Every day after school., **Sample D:** write, **5.** list ways seeds move, **6.** find a library book about seeds, **7.** drop, **8.** I have a new dog., **9.** don't, **10.** The seed ends look like a sharp fishhook., **11.** seeds, **12.** talk to a car salesperson, **13.** wash the car, **14.** The car will have two doors., **15.** Very loudly for people to hear., **16.** Correct the way it is, **17.** Thursday, June 28, **18.** Please call to find out more., **Sample E:** overe, **19.** prety, **20.** storie, **21.** ende, **22.** splashd, **23.** brushs, **24.** sed, **25.** filld, **26.** fase, **27.** toyes, **28.** parkt, **29.** livz

# Unit 9

### Practice Test 1: Pages 92–99
(Allow 40 minutes for this test.)

**Say:** Turn to Practice Test 1 on page 92. In this test, you will use your reading skills to answer questions. The test is divided into three parts. For each part there is a sample exercise. We will work each sample together. Place your marker under the first pair of sentences on page 92. This is Sample A. In this part of the test, you will solve riddles. Look at the pictures of the slide, the ladder, and the stool. Listen carefully as I read the sentences. "You can climb on it. It is made of wood." Darken the circle under the picture that shows something the sentences tell about.

**Say:** You should have darkened the circle under the picture of the ladder. A ladder is something that you can climb on, and it is made of wood. You do not climb on a slide or a stool. Also, slides and stools are often made of metal and not wood.

**Say:** Now you will solve more riddles. Put your marker under the next row for number 1. Do numbers 1 through 7 just as you did Sample A. Darken the circle under the correct answer. You may now begin. (Allow the child 10 minutes to find and mark the answers.)

**Say:** Now go to page 93 and find the samples at the top of the page. In the next part of the test, you will find words that best complete sentences. Place your marker under the first row of words under the picture. This is Sample B. Study the picture. Listen as I read the first sentence. "Gino is riding his big brother's—*tricycle … bicycle … wagon.*" Darken the circle under the word that best completes the sentence.

**Say:** Now place your marker under the second row of words under the picture. This is Sample C. Now listen carefully as I read the second sentence. "Gino splashed water on Ms. Zamora's—*dress … hat … car.*" Darken the circle under the word that best completes the sentence.

**Say:** For Sample B, the first sentence, you should have darkened the circle under the word *bicycle*. The picture shows that Gino is riding a bicycle. For Sample C, the second sentence, you should have darkened the circle under the word *dress*. The picture shows that Ms. Zamora's dress has been splashed with water.

**Say:** Now you will find more words that best complete sentences. Place your marker under the row of words under the next picture for number 8. Do numbers 8 through 14 just as you did Samples B and C. Darken the circle under the correct answer. You have 10 minutes to complete this part of the test. You may now begin.

**Say:** Now turn to page 94 and find Sample D. In the last part of the test, you will answer questions about stories that you read. Put your marker under the first row. This is Sample D. Read the story. Then, read the question and the answer choices that follow. "What were Toni and her dad doing?" *Eating seeds … watering flowers … planting a garden.* Darken the circle beside the correct answer.

**Say:** You should have darkened the circle beside the last answer choice, *planting a garden.* You can tell from the story that Toni and her dad are planting and watering seeds for a garden. In the last sentence Toni says that they will have good things to eat. This tells you that they are planting a garden. They are not eating seeds or watering flowers.

**Say:** Now you will answer more questions about stories that you read. Place your marker under the next row, the one that has the title, "Maria's Party." Do numbers 15 through 38 just as you did Sample D. Read each story and each question carefully. Darken the circle beside the correct answer. If no choices are given, write your answer on the lines. You have 20 minutes to complete this part of the test. You may now begin.

## Answers: Pages 92–99

**Sample A:** ladder, **1.** table, **2.** tiger, **3.** rocking horse, **4.** spaceship, **5.** bear, **6.** violin, **7.** duck, **Sample B:** bicycle, **Sample C:** dress, **8.** baby, **9.** bottle, **10.** classroom, **11.** a teacher, **12.** fishing pole, **13.** fish, **14.** smiling, **Sample D:** planting a garden, **15.** She blew up balloons., **16.** gifts, **17.** on the cake, **18.** a birthday party, **19.** in many places in the world, **20.** there are many different kinds of butterflies, **21.** after eating for many months, **22.** Their colors are the same as the colors of a tree., **23.** things to do at the dude ranch, **24.** Trail Ride, **25.** 2 P.M., **26.** Dinner and Barn Dance, **27.** a trip to the circus, **28.** two, **29.** She thought the clown was funny., **30.** enjoyed the circus, **31.** living on a farm, **32.** swimming, **33.** a name, **34.** enjoys living on the farm, **35.** to see snow, **36.** his aunt and uncle, **37.** snowman, **38.** It had snowed the night before.

# Unit 10

## Practice Test 2: Pages 100–105

(Allow 50 minutes for this test.)

**Say:** Turn to Practice Test 2 on page 100. In this test, you will use your reading vocabulary and word study skills to answer questions. Look at Sample A. Study the picture. There is one word in this row that tells about something in the picture. Look at the words: *boot … boat … plane.* Darken the circle under the word that tells about the picture.

**Say:** You should have darkened the circle under the word *boat* because the picture shows a submarine, which is a kind of boat.

**Say:** Now place your marker under Sample B. Look at the words: *above … beyond … below.* Darken the circle under the word that tells about the picture.

**Say:** You should have darkened the circle under the word *below* because the picture shows a submarine below the surface of the water.

**Say:** Now place your marker under Sample C. Look at the words: *sea … sand … shore.* Darken the circle under the word that tells about the picture.

**Say:** You should have darkened the circle under the word *sea* because the picture shows a submarine in the sea.

**Say:** Now you will finish the test on your own. Place your marker under the next row of words under the picture for number 1. Do numbers 1 through 15 just as you did the samples. Darken the circle under the correct answer. You may now begin.

**Say:** Now turn to page 101. In this part of the test, you will find compound words. Look at Sample D. Look at the words: *lovely … ladybug …* and *magic.* Which of these words is made up of two words? Darken the circle beside the compound word.

**Say:** You should have darkened the circle beside *ladybug* because *ladybug* is a compound word made up of the words *lady* and *bug.*

**Say:** Now you will find more compound words. Put your marker under the group of words in number 16. Do numbers 16 through 26 just as you did Sample D. Darken the circle beside the correct answer. You may now begin.

**Say:** Now turn to page 102. In the next part of the test, you will match printed words with words that you hear. Look at the words: *open … openly … opening.* These words are similar, but they do not have the same ending. I will say a word and read it in a sentence. Listen carefully. Darken the circle beside the word *open.* What time does the store *open*? *Open.*

**Say:** You should have darkened the circle beside the first word, *open.* Although *open* is a part of each word, *open* is the word that you heard.

**Say:** Now you will match more printed words with words that you hear. Put your marker under the group of words in number 27. You will do numbers 27 through 31 just as you did Sample E. Listen carefully to the word and the sentence. Then, darken the circle beside the correct answer.

**Say:**

27. Darken the circle beside the word *weekly.* They have a *weekly* meeting. *Weekly.*

28. Place your marker under the next group of words. Darken the circle beside the word *peeking.* Maura was *peeking* around the corner. *Peeking.*

29. Place your marker under the next group of words. Darken the circle beside the word *teaches.* Mr. Rostov *teaches* ballet. *Teaches.*

30. Place your marker under the next group of words. Darken the circle beside the word *masked.* I saw a movie about a *masked* hero. *Masked.*

31. Place your marker under the last group of words in the first column. Darken the circle beside the word *buys.* Dad *buys* shoes in that store. *Buys.*

**Say:** Now look at Sample F at the top of the second column. In this part of the test, you will find contractions. Look at the words: *he'll … he's … he'd.* Each of these words is a contraction. I will say two words and use them in a sentence. You will find the contraction that has the same meaning as the two words I say. Listen carefully. Darken the circle beside the word that means *he will. He will* visit us again soon. *He will.*

**Say:** You should have darkened the circle beside *he'll,* because *he'll* is the contraction of the words *he will.*

**Say:** Now you will find more contractions. Put your marker under the group of words in number 32. You will do numbers 32 through 36 just as you did Sample F. Listen carefully to the two words and the sentence. Then, darken the circle beside the correct answer.

**Say:**

32. Darken the circle beside the word that means *she would. She would* like to go swimming. *She would.*

33. Place your marker under the next group of words. Darken the circle beside the word that means *cannot.* Mrs. Estrada *cannot* stop talking about that book. *Cannot.*

34. Place your marker under the next group of words. Darken the circle beside the word that means *will not.* Justin *will not* be here today. *Will not.*

35. Place your marker under the next group of words. Darken the circle beside the word that means *we will. We will* have a wonderful time at the park. *We will.*

36. Place your marker under the last group of words on the page. Darken the circle beside the word that means *I would. I would* like to try karate. *I would.*

**Say:** Now go to page 103. In this part of the test, you will match words that have the same sound or sounds as words that you hear. Look at Sample G. Look at the word *glad* and the three answer choices. Notice that the *g* and the *l* in *glad* are underlined. Think about the sound the *g* and *l* in *glad* makes. Now listen carefully. Darken the circle below the word that has the same sound as the underlined *gl* in *glad.*

**Say:** You should have darkened the circle below *glue,* because *glue* has the same sound as the underlined letters *gl* in *glad.*

**Say:** Now you will match more words that have the same sound or sounds as words that you hear. Put your marker under the row of words in number 37. You will do numbers 37 through 48 just as you did Sample G. Listen carefully as I read each word. Then, darken the circle under the correct answer.

**Say:**

37. Darken the circle under the word that has the same sound as the underlined letter in *lunch … lunch.*

38. Place your marker under the next row of words. Darken the circle under the word that has the same sound as the underlined letter in *bat … bat.*

39. Place your marker under the next row of words. Darken the circle under the word that has the same sound as the underlined letter in *hiss … hiss.*

40. Place your marker under the next row of words. Darken the circle under the word that has the same sounds as the underlined letters in *state … state.*

41. Place your marker under the next row of words. Darken the circle under the word that has the same sound as the underlined letter in *circle … circle.*

42. Place your marker under the next row of words. Darken the circle under the word that has the same sound as the underlined letters in *those … those*.

43. Move to the top of the second column. Darken the circle under the word that has the same sound as the underlined letters in *clear … clear*.

44. Place your marker under the next row of words. Darken the circle under the word that has the same sound as the underlined letters in *door … door*.

45. Place your marker under the next row of words. Darken the circle under the word that has the same sound as the underlined letters in *curl … curl*.

46. Place your marker under the next row of words on the page. Darken the circle under the word that has the same sound as the underlined letter in *mouse … mouse*.

47. Place your marker under the next row of words. Darken the circle under the word that has the same sound as the underlined letter in *give … give*.

48. Place your marker under the last row of words on the page. Darken the circle under the word that has the same sound as the underlined letters in *boat … boat*.

Say: Turn to page 104. In this part of this test, you will match names of pictures with words that have the same consonant sounds. Look at the pictures in Sample H. There are pictures of a horse, a truck, and a fork. Which picture begins with the same sound as *hold … hold*?

Say: You should have darkened the circle under the picture of the horse because the words *horse* and *hold* begin with the same sound.

Say: Now you will match more consonant sounds. Listen carefully. Put your marker on number 49. Darken the circle under the correct answer as I read each question aloud.

49. Darken the circle under the picture whose name ends with the same sound as *trash . . . trash*.

50. Put your marker on the next row of words. Darken the circle under the word that begins with the same sounds as *thick … thick*.

51. Put your marker on the next row of words. Darken the circle under the word that ends with the same sounds as *short … short*.

52. Put your marker on the next row of words. Darken the circle under the word that has the same consonant sound in the middle as *ribbon … ribbon*.

Say:

53. Move to the top of the next column. Now you will find rhyming words. Put your marker on number 53.

Darken the circle under the picture whose name rhymes with *think … think*.

54. Put your marker on the next row of pictures. Darken the circle under the picture whose name rhymes with *rail … rail*.

55. Put your marker on the next row of words. Darken the circle under the word that rhymes with *hood … hood*.

56. Put your marker on the last row of words. Darken the circle under the word that rhymes with *cheese … cheese*.

Say: Now turn to page 105. In this part of the test you will add suffixes, or word endings, to make new words.

57. Put your marker on number 57. Look at the word *hard*. Darken the circle under the ending that can be added to the word *hard* to make a new word.

58. Look at the word *bring* in row 58. Darken the circle under the ending that can be added to make a new word.

59. Look at the word *catch* in row 59. Darken the circle under the ending that can be added to make a new word.

60. Look at the word *new* in row 60. Darken the circle under the ending that can be added to make a new word.

61. Look at the word *miss* in row 61. Darken the circle under the ending that can be added to make a new word.

62. Look at the word *good* in row 62. Darken the circle under the ending that can be added to make a new word.

## Answers: Pages 100–105

**Sample A:** boat, **Sample B:** below, **Sample C:** sea, **1.** build, **2.** blocks, **3.** careful, **4.** feed, **5.** goats, **6.** farm, **7.** play, **8.** baseball, **9.** park, **10.** jumping, **11.** rope, **12.** play, **13.** car, **14.** wash, **15.** soap, **Sample D:** ladybug, **16.** afternoon, **17.** footsteps, **18.** haircut, **19.** ponytail, **20.** rooftop, **21.** sailboat, **22.** baseball, **23.** daytime, **24.** beehive, **25.** doorbell, **26.** cupcake, **Sample E:** open, **27.** weekly, **28.** peeking, **29.** teaches, **30.** masked, **31.** buys, **Sample F:** he'll, **32.** she'd, **33.** can't, **34.** won't, **35.** we'll, **36.** I'd, **Sample G:** glue, **37.** tummy, **38.** ladder, **39.** will, **40.** first, **41.** center, **42.** there, **43.** close, **44.** wore, **45.** shirt, **46.** lamb, **47.** forget, **48.** open, **Sample H:** horse, **49.** brush, **50.** think, **51.** hurt, **52.** rabbit, **53.** man drinking, **54.** nail, **55.** wood, **56.** please, **57.** ly, **58.** ing, **59.** er, **60.** est, **61.** ed, **62.** ness

# Unit 11

## Practice Test 3: Pages 106–112

(Allow about 40 minutes for this part of the test. Read items at a moderate, steady pace. Distribute scratch paper for the child to use to work the problems. Also distribute inch and centimeter rulers.)

**Say:** Turn to Part 1 of Practice Test 3 on page 106. In this test you will use your math skills to choose pictures and numbers that answer math problems you hear. Place your marker under the first row. This is Sample A. Now listen carefully. Darken the circle under the picture that can be folded on the dotted line so that the parts on each side of the line match exactly.

**Say:** You should have darkened the circle under the third picture. The vase is the only picture whose sides will match if it is folded on the dotted line.

**Say:** Now place your marker under the next row, the one with the picture of the marbles. This is Sample B. Listen carefully. Darken the circle for the number that tells exactly how many marbles are shown in the picture.

**Say:** You should have darkened the circle under the second number, 23. There are 23 marbles in the picture.

**Say:** Now you will choose more pictures and numbers that answer math problems. Listen carefully to each problem. Then, choose your answer from the pictures or numbers given in the row. If no choices are given, write your answer on the lines. Place your marker under the row for number 1. (Say each number only once.)

**Say:**

1. Darken the circle under the number *three hundred fifteen*.

2. Place your marker under the next row. Darken the circle under the box that has the most number of hearts.

3. Place your marker under the next row. There are six stacks of blocks and some extra blocks. Darken the circle under the number that tells how many blocks there are altogether.

4. Place your marker under the last row on the page. Darken the circle under the bird that is fourth from the cage.

**Say:** Now go to page 107. Now we will continue the test. Place your marker under the first row for number 5.

5. Look at the numbers in the box. Darken the circle under the number that means the same as fifty plus eight.

6. Place your marker under the next row. Look at the number on the gift. Darken the circle under the number that is ten less than the number on the gift.

7. Place your marker under the next row. Be sure to move your marker so you can see all of the answer choices. Look at the number sentence in the box. Darken the circle under the number sentence that is in the same fact family.

8. Place your marker under the next row. Write the number that goes in the box to make the number sentence correct.

9. Place your marker under the next row. Darken the circle under the number that is more than forty-five and less than sixty-nine.

10. Place your marker under the last row on the page. Darken the circle under the two numbers that have a seven in the ones place.

**Say:** Now turn to page 108. Now we will continue the test. Place your marker under the first row, number 11.

11. Look at the numbers in the box. Darken the circle under the numbers that mean the same as three plus four.

12. Place your marker under the next row for number 12. Darken the circle under the shape that has one sixth shaded.

13. Place your marker under the next row. Darken the circle under the square that is divided into four equal parts.

14. Place your marker under the next row. Darken the circle under the group that shows one third of the apples eaten.

15. Place your marker under the last row on the page. In this item, we will count by fives. Write the number that belongs in the empty box.

**Say:** Now go to page 109. Now we will continue the test. Place your marker under the first row, number 16. Look at the graph. It shows the number of boxes of seeds sold. You will use this graph to answer numbers 16 and 17.

16. Place your marker under the row for number 16. Look at the graph. Darken the circle under the number that shows the boxes of flower seeds sold.

17. Place your marker under the next row. Look at the graph again. Darken the circle under the picture that stands for the fewest boxes of seeds sold.

18. Place your marker under the next row. Maria lives in an apartment building. Darken the circle under the picture that shows Maria's door if she lives in apartment twenty-two.

19. Place your marker under the next row. Monica makes a tally chart to show the supplies in her school box. Write the number that shows how many crayons Monica has in her school box.

20. Place your marker under the last row on the page. Look at the pattern of fruit. Darken the circle under the piece of fruit that comes next in the pattern.

**Say:** Now go to page 110. Now we will continue the test. Place your marker under the first row, number 21.

21. Look at the figure in the box. Darken the circle under the figure in the row that is exactly the same as the figure in the box.

22. Place your marker under the next row. Darken the circle under the picture that shows a triangle inside a square.

23. Place your marker under the next row. Listen carefully. Yukio played a game with tile shapes. She put eight diamonds, two squares, one triangle, and four circles into a box. If Yukio picks one shape out of the box without looking, which shape will Yukio most likely pick? She put into a box eight diamonds, two squares, one triangle, and four circles. Darken the circle under the shape Yukio will most likely pick from the box.

24. Place your marker under the next row. Darken the circle under the number that tells about how many fish long the aquarium is.

25. Place your marker under the last row on the page. Use your inch ruler to answer the problem. Listen carefully. Write the number that tells the length of the rope.

**Say:** Now go to page 111. Now we will continue the test. Place your marker under the first row, number 26.

26. Terry cleaned the inside of the car. He found a total of five cents. Darken the circle beside the group of coins that shows five cents.

27. Place your marker under the next row. Calvin is baking cookies. Darken the circle under the best measurement to use in baking cookies.

28. Place your marker under the last row on the page. Look at the clock. Chou has piano lessons every Saturday at the time shown on this clock. Darken the circle under the number that tells the time when Chou has piano lessons each Saturday.

**Say:** Now turn to page 112. Now we will continue the test. Place your marker under the first row, number 29.

29. Listen to this riddle about a number. I am thinking of a number that is between forty-one and sixty. It has a five in it. What number am I thinking of? It is between forty-one and sixty and it has a five in it. Darken the circle under the number that I am thinking of.

30. Place your marker under the next row. Look at the skunks. Five skunks are standing together. Two more skunks join them. How many skunks are there altogether? Darken the circle under the number sentence that shows how to find the number of skunks altogether.

31. Place your marker under the next row. Listen to this riddle about a number. I am thinking of a number that is less than twenty-two. You say its name when you count by twos. It has an eight in it. What number am I thinking of? It is less than twenty-two, you say its name when you count by twos, and it has an eight in it. Darken the circle under the number that I am thinking of.

32. Place your marker under the last row on the page. Look at the calendar. Juan's birthday is the third Tuesday in October. Write the number of the date for the third Tuesday in October.

## Answers: Pages 106–112
**Sample A:** vase, **Sample B:** 23, **1.** 315,
**2.** The second circle should be darkened., **3.** 66,
**4.** The second circle should be darkened., **5.** 58,
**6.** 32, **7.** 6 − 5 = 1, **8.** 8, **9.** 52, **10.** 27, 17, **11.** 4 + 3,
**12.** The fourth circle should be darkened., **13.** The third circle should be darkened., **14.** The first circle should be darkened., **15.** 40, **16.** 5, **17.** The second circle should be darkened., **18.** The second circle should be darkened., **19.** 8, **20.** The third circle should be darkened., **21.** The third circle should be darkened., **22.** The first circle should be darkened., **23.** The first circle should be darkened., **24.** 6, **25.** 5 inches, **26.** The first circle should be darkened., **27.** cups, **28.** 3:30, **29.** 54, **30.** 5 + 2 =, **31.** 18, **32.** 21

## Practice Test 3:  Part 2: Pages 113–116
(Allow about 30 minutes for this part of the test. Read items at a moderate, steady pace. Distribute scratch paper for the child to use to work the problems.)
**Say:** Turn to page 113. In this part of the test you will add and subtract numbers that answer math problems you hear or read. This section is divided into two parts. There is a sample for each part. We will work the samples together. Place your marker under the first row, the one with the pictures of the leaves. This is Sample C. Now listen carefully. Jason collects leaves. Yesterday he went hiking through the woods near the lake. He found five oak

leaves. Then, he found eight maple leaves. How many leaves did he find altogether? Darken the circle under the number that tells how many leaves Jason found altogether. If the correct answer is not given, darken the circle for *NH, not here.*

**Say:** You should have darkened the circle under the second number, 13. Jason found five leaves and then he found eight leaves. If you add these together, five plus eight equals 13.

**Say:** Now place your marker under the next row. This is Sample D. You are asked to add nine and two. Use the scratch paper to work the problem. Write the correct answer on the lines.

**Say:** You should have written 11. Nine plus two equals eleven.

**Say:** Now you will add and subtract more numbers that answer math problems you hear or read. Listen carefully to each problem. Then, darken the circle for the correct answer. If the correct answer is not given, darken the circle for *NH, not here.* If no choices are given, write your answer on the lines. Place your marker under the row for number 1. (Say each number only once.)

**Say:**

1. Listen carefully to this story. Ellen likes rag dolls. She had seven rag dolls. For her birthday she received three more rag dolls. How many rag dolls does she now have altogether? Darken the circle under the number that tells how many rag dolls she has altogether.

2. Place your marker under the last row on the page. The pet store is having a fish sale. There are twenty fish in one tank. There are fifteen fish in another tank. How many fish are there in all? Darken the circle under the number that tells how many fish there are in all.

**Say:** Now turn to page 114. Now we will continue the test. Place your marker under the first row for number 3. Now listen carefully.

3. Rita checked out seven books from the library. She read four the first day. How many books does she have left to read? Write the number that tells how many books she has left to read.

4. Place your marker under the next row for number 4. Chi-Hun went to the airport. He saw sixteen airplanes. He saw six helicopters. How many more airplanes than helicopters did he see? Darken the circle under the number that tells how many more airplanes than helicopters Chi-Hun saw.

5. Place your marker under the next row for number 5. There are thirty-seven balls in the gym. Coach Ellis uses four balls for a game. How many balls are left? Darken the circle under the number that tells how many balls are left.

6. Place your marker under the last row on the page. Ms. Todd bought a package of fifty dinosaur stickers. She gave away thirty of the stickers to the students in her class. How many dinosaur stickers does she have left? Darken the circle under the number that tells how many dinosaur stickers are left.

**Say:** Now go to page 115. In this part of the test, you will add or subtract numbers. Do numbers 7 through 26 on your own. Look at each problem carefully. Work the problem on the scratch paper. Then, darken the circle for the correct answer. If no choices are given, write your answer on the lines. If the correct answer is not given, darken the circle for *NH, not here.* You may now begin. (Allow students 20 minutes to find and mark or write their answers.)

**Answers: Pages 113–116**
**Sample C:** 13, **Sample D:** 11, **1.** 10, **2.** 35, **3.** 3, **4.** 10, **5.** 33, **6.** 20, **7.** NH, **8.** 10, **9.** 15, **10.** NH, **11.** 55, **12.** 89, **13.** 72, **14.** 48, **15.** 18, **16.** 88, **17.** 1, **18.** 7, **19.** 7, **20.** 41, **21.** NH, **22.** 11, **23.** 50, **24.** 19, **25.** 9, **26.** 310

# Unit 12

## Practice Test 4: Pages 117–119

(Allow 25 minutes for this test.)

**Say:** Turn to page 117. In this test, you will use your listening skills to answer questions. This test is divided into three parts. For each part there is a sample exercise. We will work each sample together. Place your marker under the first row. This is Sample A. In this part of the test, you will find the words that best complete sentences. I will read part of a sentence and three words. You will find the word that best completes the sentence. Look at the three words in Sample A. Listen carefully. The part of your body you use to think with is your—*forehead … brain … heart*. Darken the circle beside the word that best completes the sentence.

**Say:** You should have darkened the circle beside *brain*. The brain is the part of your body you use to think with.

**Say:** Now you will find more words that best complete sentences. Put your marker under number 1. Make sure you can see all the answer choices. You will do numbers 1 through 12 just as you did Sample A. Listen carefully to the sentence and the three answer choices. Then, darken the circle beside the correct answer. (Say each item only once.)

**Say:**

1. My dog's tricks might *amaze* you. To amaze is to—*surprise … upset … scare*.

2. Place your marker under the next row. When Grandpa rescued a baby, he was called a *hero*. A hero is someone who does something—*brave … easy … quickly*.

3. Place your marker under the next row. After a bowl of milk, the kitten was *content*. Another word for content is—*happy … worried … funny*.

4. Place your marker under the next row. It is Santos' turn to *raise* the flag. To raise is to—*bring down … lift … fold*.

5. Place your marker under the next row. Lee's sister has a cold, but Lee is not *ill*. Another word for ill is—*lazy … sick … absent*.

6. Place your marker under the next row. We sat at the *back* of the bus. Another name for the back is the—*front … rear … middle*.

**Say:**

7. Go to the top of the next column. Place your marker under number 7. Uncle Jeff will *manage* the new store. To manage is to—*take care of … leave … talk about*.

8. Place your marker under the next row. He made a *sketch* of the town. A sketch is a—*song … book … drawing*.

9. Place your marker under the next row. This is where we *switch* trains. To switch is to—*change … tear … count*.

10. Place your marker under the next row. The clown told a *foolish* joke. Another word for foolish is—*excited … angry … silly*.

11. Place your marker under the next row. Luke is waiting for us *where the two streets meet*. A place where two streets meet is called—*an avenue … a corner … a road*.

12. Place your marker under the last row. Tia had to *run quickly* to get her books. To run quickly is to—*dash … wander … slide*.

**Say:** Now turn to page 118. Place your marker under Sample B. In this part of the test, you will choose pictures that answer questions. Study the pictures. I will read a story and then ask a question. You will find the picture that best answers the question. Listen carefully. Some animals have fur. Some animals have feathers. What animal does not have fur or feathers? Is it—*the bird … the bear …* or *the fish*? Darken the circle under the picture of the correct answer.

**Say:** You should have darkened the circle under the fish. A fish does not have fur or feathers.

**Say:** Now you will choose more pictures that best answer questions. Put your marker under number 13. Make sure you can see all the answer choices. You will do numbers 13 through 21 just as you did Sample B. Listen carefully to the story and the question. Then, darken the circle under the picture for each correct answer. (Say each item only once.)

**Say:** Listen to this story. Then, answer the question. When Juan got home from school, he played with his dog, Scooter. They played until almost dark, when Juan's mother told him that it was time to come in and get ready for dinner.

13. What did Juan do to get ready for dinner? Did he—*wash his hands … feed the dog …* or *go to bed*?

**Say:** Place your marker under the next row. Listen to this story. You will answer two questions. Ryan's mother came home from the hospital with his baby sister, Christine. Ryan carried the suitcase into the house. Then, Ryan helped wash the baby. Then, Ryan's mother told him that he could feed Christine. He sat in the rocking chair and gave Christine her bottle.

14. What did Ryan do first? Did he—*help wash the baby ... carry the suitcase ... feed the baby*?

15. Ryan fed his baby sister in—*the high chair ... the rocking chair ... his arms*.

**Say:** Place your marker under the next row. Listen to this story. There is one question. Anita and her family went camping. The family decided to swim in the lake before lunch. They put their lunch basket on the picnic table. Anita and her family did not know that a mother bear and her cubs were nearby.

16. Darken the circle under the picture that shows what Anita and her family found when they returned to the picnic table.

**Say:** Place your marker under the next row. Listen to this story. There are two questions to answer. Olivia and her mother went shopping. Olivia found a rack of hats and tried some on. Her mother laughed when Olivia tried on a hat that was so big it covered her eyes. When Olivia and her mother got home, it looked as if it might rain. "Please get my purse, Olivia, and take it into the house," said her mother. "And please make sure that rain can't get into the car."

17. Darken the circle under the picture that shows what Olivia looked like when her mother laughed.

18. Place your marker under the next row. What did Olivia do so that rain would not get into the car? Did she—*open the door ... roll up the window ... or get the purse*?

**Say:** Place your marker under the next row. Listen to this story. Then, answer the question. Animals have different things that they use to protect themselves. Some, like deer and goats, have horns. Others have sharp teeth.

19. Something else animals have to protect themselves is—*an eye ... claws ... a log*.

**Say:** Place your marker under the next row. Listen to this story. Every weekend, Andrew has three jobs he has to do before he can play. First, he waters his mother's plants. Next, he washes the dishes. Then, he helps his dad by raking the leaves in the yard. Now Andrew can go out and play.

20. Darken the circle under the picture that shows the first job Andrew does.

**Say:** Place your marker under the last row. Listen to this story. Then, answer the question. Today is Gina's seventh birthday. Her aunt gave her a pair of dancing shoes. Her uncle made her a dollhouse. Her stepfather also gave her a wonderful present, a fluffy white poodle named Snowball.

21. What did Gina receive from her aunt? Was it—*dancing shoes ... a poodle ... or a dollhouse*?

**Say:** Now go to page 119. Place your marker under Sample C. In this part of the test, you will choose the words that best answer questions. I will read a story and then ask a question. You will choose the best answer to the question. Patrick and his mother had just stepped out of their car when a heavy rain began to pour down. "Stand under that awning," Patrick's mother said. "I have to get something from the car so we won't get wet." Now listen carefully. Patrick's mother went to the car to get—*a flag ... an umbrella ... a sandwich*. Darken the circle beside the words that best answer the question.

**Say:** You should have darkened the circle beside an umbrella. Patrick's mother went to the car to get an umbrella because it was raining.

**Say:** Now you will choose more words that best answer questions. Put your marker under number 22. Make sure you can see all the answer choices. You will do numbers 22 through 34 just as you did Sample C. Listen carefully to the story and the question. Then, darken the circle beside each correct answer.

**Say:** Listen carefully as I read this story. You will answer two questions.

Everyone enjoys the Plum Creek Library. In the mornings, retired people meet there to discuss books they have read. During the afternoons, young children check out books, listen to stories, and see puppet plays. In the evenings, students come there to study and do research.

22. Retired people meet at the library to—*discuss books ... play softball ... put on puppet plays*.

23. Place your marker under the next row. Students use the library to do research and—*sleep ... cook ... study*.

**Say:** Now put your marker under number 24. Listen carefully as I read this story. You will answer two questions. Mr. and Mrs. Shah live in Chicago. They are excited because they are going on a trip. First, they will drive their car to the airport. Then, they will fly in a plane to Seattle. From there, they will sail on a boat to Alaska. In Alaska, they will take a train to see different parts of the state.

24. Mr. and Mrs. Shah are going on a trip to—*California ... Hawaii ... Alaska*.

25. Place your marker under the next row. The first thing they will do is—*sail on a boat ... ride in a car ... fly in a plane*.

**Say:** Now put your marker under number 26. Listen carefully as I read this story. You will answer two questions. Rolanda loves to visit her grandmother and grandfather in Mexico. She goes there with her parents every summer. She sees all her aunts and uncles and cousins. When Rolanda and her family arrive, there is a big celebration. Then, over the next few weeks, the family goes to parks, museums, and restaurants. Rolanda's favorite part is listening to her grandparents tell stories about the family. When it is time to go home, Rolanda is sad. But she knows that she'll be coming back next year.

26. There is a big celebration because Rolanda and her parents—*come to visit ... are leaving ... have a birthday.*

27. Place your marker under the next row. A good name for this story would be—*"Rolanda and Her Aunts"..."Celebrations in Mexico"..."Rolanda's Trips to Mexico."*

**Say:** Now put your marker under number 28 at the top of the next column. Listen carefully as I read this story. You will answer one question. Manuel told Larry that his turtle could beat Larry's dog in a race. Larry didn't believe him, so they decided to see what would happen. The dog ran very fast, and the turtle crawled very slowly. But just before the dog reached the finish line, he saw another dog and ran off to play with it. The turtle kept crawling until he reached the finish line.

28. The dog didn't finish the race because he—*became tired ... stumbled and fell ... ran off to play.*

**Say:** Now put your marker on number 29. Listen carefully as I read this story. You will answer three questions. Wesley and Beth were building a snow friend. First, they made three balls of snow. Then, they stacked up the snowballs. They found two sticks for arms. They made a face with a carrot nose and raisin eyes and mouth. They put a western hat on top of their snow person's head. "I guess we can call it a snow cowpoke," said Beth.

29. Beth and Wesley are playing in—*sand ... snow ... dirt.*

30. Place your marker under the next row. Wesley and Beth called their snow friend a cowpoke because of its—*hat ... nose ... arms.*

31. Place your marker under the next row. After building their snow friend, Beth and Wesley probably felt—*afraid ... proud ... angry.*

**Say:** Now put your marker on number 32. Listen carefully as I read this story. You will answer three questions. Robin's aunt and uncle took her to a big theme park. The first thing Robin wanted to do was see the princess's castle. Then, they rode several rides. Robin's favorite ride took them underwater. Cartoon characters waved at them as they walked around the park. The first day ended with a big parade and fireworks. As they walked to their hotel room, Robin thanked her aunt and uncle for their wonderful gift.

32. Place your marker under the next row. The wonderful gift Robin's aunt and uncle gave her was a—*trip to the theme park ... gold bracelet ... new sweater.*

33. Place your marker under the next row. The first thing Robin wanted to see was the—*cartoon characters ... underwater ride ... princess's castle.*

34. Place your marker under the next row. The cartoon characters in the park—*took Robin on a ride ... waved at Robin ... showed Robin a castle.*

## Answers: Pages 117–119
**Sample A:** brain, **1.** surprise, **2.** brave, **3.** happy, **4.** lift, **5.** sick, **6.** rear, **7.** take care of, **8.** drawing, **9.** change, **10.** silly, **11.** a corner, **12.** dash, **Sample B:** fish, **13.** first picture, **14.** second picture, **15.** second picture, **16.** second picture, **17.** first picture, **18.** second picture, **19.** second picture, **20.** third picture, **21.** first picture, **Sample C:** an umbrella, **22.** discuss books, **23.** study, **24.** Alaska, **25.** ride in a car, **26.** come to visit, **27.** "Rolanda's Trips to Mexico," **28.** ran off to play, **29.** snow, **30.** hat, **31.** proud, **32.** trip to the theme park, **33.** princess's castle, **34.** waved at Robin

# Unit 13

(Allow 40 minutes for this test. Read items at a moderate, steady pace.)

**Say:** Turn to page 120. In this test, you will choose pictures that answer questions about stories you hear. Place your marker under the first row. This is Sample A. Now listen carefully. Forest Lane is an old country road. There is a covered bridge on Forest Lane that is only wide enough for one car to drive across at a time. Darken the circle for the picture that shows the bridge on Forest Lane.

**Say:** You should have darkened the circle for the first picture. The first picture shows a bridge that is only wide enough for one car to drive across at a time.

**Say:** Now you will choose more pictures that answer questions about stories you hear. Listen carefully to each story. Then, choose your answer from the pictures given in the row. Place your marker under the next row.

**Say:**

1. Every morning before school, Lita eats a good breakfast. After breakfast, she always brushes her teeth. Next, she dresses and combs her hair. Then, she is ready to walk to the school bus stop. Darken the circle for the picture that shows what Lita does first each morning.

2. Place your marker under the next row. Rudy the goldfish lives in a fishbowl. Once Rudy lived in a sparkling stream in the woods. There he liked to hang in the trees near the stream. Darken the circle for the picture that shows something that could not happen.

3. Place your marker under the next row. Sam and Rolando were walking in the woods one night. As they passed under a tree, Rolando felt something sticky on his face. He wiped his face to get it off. Darken the circle for the picture that shows what Rolando felt on his face.

4. Place your marker under the last row on the page. Listen to this poem:

We looked all around for Richard's toy bear.

We finally found it behind a _____ .

Darken the circle for the picture that will rhyme with the poem.

**Say:** Now go to page 121. In this part of the test, you will answer questions about stories you hear. Listen carefully to the story and questions. Then, choose your answer from the words and sentences given.

Place your marker under the first row. Be sure to move your marker so you can see all the answer choices. This is Sample B. Look at the picture under the title "Holiday Fun" while I read you a story about Aggie. Aggie's teacher has asked the class to write a story telling about their favorite holiday. Aggie's favorite holiday is the Fourth of July. What idea will Aggie not use in her story? Is it—*Watch fireworks … Open presents …* or *Go on a picnic*? Darken the circle under the idea Aggie will not use in her story.

**Say:** You should have darkened the circle for the second answer, *Open presents*. Most people do not open presents on the Fourth of July.

**Say:** Now place your marker under the next row. This is Sample C. Listen carefully to the beginning of Aggie's story. Read it silently to yourself as I read it out loud.

I like the Fourth of July best.

My family and I like to watch the parade.

After the parade, we go to the park.

To have a picnic.

Which group of words is not a complete sentence? Is it—*I like the Fourth of July best. … After the parade, we go to the park. …* or *To have a picnic.*? Darken the circle next to the words that do not make a complete sentence.

**Say:** You should have darkened the circle for the last group of words. *To have a picnic* is not a complete sentence.

**Say:** Now place your marker under the next row. This is Sample D. Listen to the last part of Aggie's story. Read it silently to yourself as I read it out loud.

We <u>watches</u> the fireworks at night.

The colors light up the sky.

Look at the underlined word. Did Aggie use the right word? Should she write—*watch … watching … *or is the underlined word *Correct the way it is*? Darken the circle for the way Aggie should write the underlined word.

**Say:** You should have darkened the circle for the first word, *watch*. This is the correct word to use. The sentence should read, *We watch the fireworks at night.*

**Say:** Now turn to page 122. Now we will continue the test. You will find more words and sentences that answer questions about stories you hear. Listen carefully to each story. Then, choose your answer from the words and sentences given. Look at the picture under the title "The Pool Party" while I read you a story about Matt. Matt is having a pool party at his house. He is sending invitations to all of his friends. Place your marker under the first row. Be sure to move your marker so you can see all the answer choices.

5. Matt used these words in his invitation: *when*, *wish*, *water*. He wanted to look them up in a dictionary to make sure he spelled them correctly. Darken the circle for the word that would be listed first in alphabetical (ABC) order in the dictionary.

6. Place your marker under the next row. What information will Matt not put in his invitations? Is it— *the time the party begins … the size of the pool …* or *his house number and street name*? Darken the circle next to the information Matt will not put in the invitation.

**Say:** Now place your marker under the next row. Look at the beginning of an invitation Matt wrote. Read it silently to yourself as I read it out loud.

Dear Sam,

I am having a pool party.

It will be this <u>Friday, August 19</u>.
       (1)

Come to my house at 359 Pine Road.

<u>We will much fun have</u>.
      (2)

**Say:** Now you will answer some questions. Place your marker under the next row.

7. Look at the underlined words with the number 1 under them. How should Matt write these words? Should he write—*friday, august 19 … friday, August 19 …* or is the group of the underlined words *Correct the way it is*? Darken the circle for the way Matt should write the underlined words.

8. Place your marker under the last row on the page. Look at the underlined sentence with the number 2 under it. How should Matt write this sentence? Should he write—*We will have much fun. … We will have fun much. …* or is the underlined sentence *Correct the way it is*? Darken the circle for the way Matt should write the underlined sentence.

**Say:** Now look at page 123. We will now continue the test. Place your marker under the first row. Listen to the rest of Matt's invitation. Read it silently to yourself as I read it out loud.

You <u>need</u> to bring a swimsuit.
     (1)

I hope to see you.

Let me know if you <u>arent</u> coming.
       (2)

Your friend,

Matt

**Say:** Now you will answer some questions. Place your marker under the next row.

9. Look at the underlined word with the number 1 under it. Did Matt use the right word? Should he write—*needing … needed …* or is it *Correct the way it is*? Darken the circle for the way the underlined word should be written.

10. Place your marker under the next row. Look at the underlined word with the number 2 under it. Did Matt use the right word? Should he write—*aren't … are'nt …* or is it *Correct the way it is*? Darken the circle for the way the underlined word should be written.

**Say:** Now I will read another story. Look at the picture under the title "Pia's Town." Now listen as I read you a story about Pia. Pia is writing a report about the things to see and do in her town. She put a Table of Contents at the front of her report. Read it silently to yourself as I read it out loud. Chapter 1 is called "Things to See" and begins on page 3. Chapter 2 is called "Things to Do" and begins on page 10. Chapter 3 is called "Places to Eat" and begins on page 17. Chapter 4 is called "Special Events" and begins on page 26. Now place your marker under the next row.

**Say:**

11. Look at the Table of Contents. What chapter would Pia use to write about a place that has dinosaur bones? Would she use—*Chapter 1 … Chapter 2 …* or *Chapter 3*? Darken the circle for the chapter Pia would use to write about a place that has dinosaur bones.

12. Place your marker under the last row on the page. Look at the Table of Contents again. Would Pia write about a place to eat pizza on—*page 10 … page 17 …* or *page 26*? Darken the circle for the page Pia will use to write about a place to eat pizza.

**Say:** Now turn to page 124. Now we will continue the test. Place your marker under the first row. Listen to what Pia wrote in her report. Read it to yourself silently as I read it out loud.

In my town, you can visit a cave.

A train takes you under the ground.

A man tells you about the cave.

As you walk on a wide path.

**Say:** Now place your marker under the next row.

13. Which group of words is not a complete sentence? Is it—*A train takes you under the ground. … A man tells you about the cave. …* or *As you walk on a wide path.*? Darken the circle next to the group of words that does not make a complete sentence.

**Say:** Now listen to what Pia wrote next in her report. Read it silently to yourself as I read it aloud.

You can also go to the library.

Each <u>tuesday</u> they have a story time.
     (1)

<u>Someone reads</u> a story to the children.
     (2)

Sometimes they have a puppet play.

**Say:** Now place your marker under the next row.

14. Look at the underlined word with the number 1 under it. How should Pia write this word? Darken the circle for the answer that shows how Pia should write the underlined word.

15. Place your marker under the last row on the page. Look at the underlined words with the number 2 under them. How should Pia write these words? Should she write—*Someone reading … Someone read …* or is the group of words *Correct the way it is*? Darken the circle for the answer that shows how Pia should write the underlined words.

**Say:** Now look at page 125. Now we will continue the test. I will read another story. Look at the picture under the title "Camp Fun" as I read you a story about Ben. It was the beginning of the school year. The teacher asked the students to write a story about what they did during the summer. Ben had gone to Camp Lakota and learned how to sail a boat. Ben decided to write about sailing the boat.

**Say:** Now you will answer a question. Place your marker under the first row.

16. Why is Ben writing a story? Is it—*to tell his friend how to sail … to tell what he did during the summer … or to tell why he went to camp*? Darken the circle next to the words that tell why Ben is writing a story.

**Say:** Now listen to what Ben wrote in his story, "Sailing at Camp." Read it silently to yourself as I read it aloud.

Sailing at Camp

I learned to sail a boat at camp.

We ate hot dogs.

First, you have to raise the sails.

The wind fills the sails.

**Say:** Now you will answer some questions. Place your marker under number 17.

17. Which sentence does not belong in the story? Is it—*I learned to sail a boat at camp. … We ate hot dogs. …* or *First, you have to raise the sails.*? Darken the circle next to the sentence that does not belong in the story.

18. Place your marker under the last row on the page. What sentence will Ben probably write next? Is it—*The wind makes the boat move. … The camp is beside a lake. …* or *The boat is big.*? Darken the circle next to the sentence that Ben will probably write next.

**Say:** Now turn to page 126. Now I will read you the next part of Ben's story. Read it silently to yourself as I read it aloud.

Sometimes the wind does not blow.

Can you guess what happens <u>then</u>
                 (1)

The boat will not move.

<u>Mr. sanchez</u>, the camp leader, must come get you.
   (2)

**Say:** Now you will answer some questions. Place your marker under the first row.

19. Look at the underlined word with the number 1 under it. Which punctuation mark should Ben write at the end of this sentence? Should he write—*a period … a question mark …* or *an exclamation point*? Darken the circle for the punctuation mark Ben should write at the end of the word.

20. Place your marker under the last row on the page. Look at the underlined words with the number 2 under them. How should Ben write these words? Where should he use capital letters? Darken the circle for the answer that shows how Ben should write these underlined words.

**Say:** Now look at page 127. In the last part of the test, you will find words that are not spelled correctly. I will read a sentence. Three of the words are listed as the answer choices. Find the word that is not spelled correctly. Now place your marker under the first row. This is Sample E. Listen carefully. *Mr. Jones read two storys (stories) to the class.* Darken the circle next to the word that is not spelled correctly.

**Say:** You should have darkened the circle for the third word. The word *stories* is not spelled with a *ys* at the end. The word should be spelled *s-t-o-r-i-e-s.*

**Say:** Now you will find more words that are not spelled correctly. Place your marker under the next row.

21. *The teacher calld (called) your name.* Darken the circle next to the word that is not spelled correctly.

22. Place your marker under the next row. *Please give hir (her) a turn.* Darken the circle next to the word that is not spelled correctly.

23. Place your marker under the next row. *Rosa was carful (careful) not to wake her father.* Darken the circle next to the word that is not spelled correctly.

24. Place your marker under the next row. *My frend (friend) is riding his bike.* Darken the circle next to the word that is not spelled correctly.

25. Place your marker under the next row. *Please pick up your toyes (toys) before you leave.* Darken the circle next to the word that is not spelled correctly.

**Say:** Now look at the top of the page. Find the next column. Place your marker under the first row.

26. *Maria fell and bumped her noze (nose).* Darken the circle next to the word that is not spelled correctly.

27. Place your marker under the next row. *The girl made three wishs (wishes).* Darken the circle next to the word that is not spelled correctly.

28. Place your marker under the next row. *Did you win first prise (prize)?* Darken the circle next to the word that is not spelled correctly.

29. Place your marker under the next row. *The children playd (played) in the sun.* Darken the circle next to the word that is not spelled correctly.

30. Place your marker under the next row. *How many dayes (days) until my birthday?* Darken the circle next to the word that is not spelled correctly.

31. Place your marker under the last row on the page. *We packt (packed) our bags for the trip.* Darken the circle next to the word that is not spelled correctly.

## Answers: Pages 120–127

**Sample A:** first picture, **1.** first picture,
**2.** third picture, **3.** first picture, **4.** third picture,
**Sample B:** Open presents, **Sample C:** To have a picnic., **Sample D:** watch, **5.** water, **6.** the size of the pool, **7.** Correct the way it is, **8.** We will have much fun., **9.** Correct the way it is, **10.** aren't, **11.** 1, **12.** 17, **13.** As you walk on a wide path., **14.** Tuesday, **15.** Correct the way it is, **16.** to tell what he did during the summer, **17.** We ate hot dogs., **18.** The wind makes the boat move., **19.** then?, **20.** Mr. Sanchez,
**Sample E:** storys, **21.** calld, **22.** hir, **23.** carful, **24.** frend, **25.** toyes, **26.** noze, **27.** wishs, **28.** prise, **29.** playd, **30.** dayes, **31.** packt